HOW TO LIVE WITH YOUR TEENAGER II:
A Question & Answer Guide for Parents

PETER H. BUNTMAN, M.S.W., ACSW
CENTER FOR FAMILY LIFE ENRICHMENT, INC.

COPYRIGHT © 1990 BY

Center For Family Life Enrichment, Inc.
3611 Farquhar Avenue, Suite 3
Los Alamitos, California 90720

All rights reserved. This book, or parts thereof, must not be used or reproduced in any manner without written permission.

Buntman, Peter H., 1943-
   How to live with your teenager II : a question and answer guide for parents / Peter H. Buntman. —
   p. cm.
   ISBN 0-9623986-0-8

   1. Parenting. 2. Teenagers. I. Title.

HQ755.85   649.1'25
                                            QBI90-352

Pages of this book are reproduced from Pages 9-14, 107-110, and 125-130 of the book *How to Live with Your Teenager; A Survivior's Handbook for Parents,* by Peter H. Buntman, M.S.W., ACSW, and Eleanor M. Saris M.Ed.

"How to Live with Your Teenager II: A Question and Answer Guide for Parents" was first published in 1990 as "Winning the Parent-Teenager Conflict Game."

SECOND PRINTING 1991
THIRD PRINTING 1992

Peter H. Buntman M.S.W., ACSW, Licensed Clinical Social Worker, specializes in counseling and therapy with teenagers (age 9 to 19) and their families.

Mr. Buntman is Director of the Center for Family Life Enrichment, Inc. Mr. Buntman and his professional associates at the Center work with parents of problem teenagers.

The Center offers full counseling facilities, as well as tutoring and after school study hall programs for teens who need help in school. The Center has offices located in Anaheim, Cerritos, Costa Mesa, Downey, Fullerton, Huntington Beach, Irvine, Lakewood, Los Alamitos, Orange, Torrance and Whittier, Califomia.

Mr. Buntman can be reached by writing

The Center for Family Life Enrichment, Inc.

3611 Farquhar Avenue Suite 3

Los Alamitos, California 90720

or by calling

(310) 596-8712 or (714) 761-0844.

Peter H. Buntman, M.S.W., ACSW, is an internationally recognized psychotherapist who specializes in working with "teenagers, teen problems, and how to solve them."

His first book, *How To Live With Your Teenager: A Survivor's Handbook for Parents,* is a leading authoritative text on adolescent behavior, and has sold well over 100,000 copies. Mr. Buntman has been interviewed on hundreds of radio and television talk shows nationwide and has been featured on a series of television documentaries aired both in Canada and the United States.

PETER H. BUNTMAN

He has been a mental health consultant to numerous federal, state, and local agencies dealing with adolescent problems.

Professionally, Mr. Buntman is a Licensed Clinical Social Worker. He is the executive director of the Center for Family Life Enrichment which has offices located throughout Orange County and Los Angeles County, California, including offices in Anaheim, Cerritos, Costa Mesa, Downey, Fullerton, Huntington Beach, Irvine, Lakewood, Los Alamitos, Orange, Torrance and Whittier, California.

Mr. Buntman is on the Affiliated Medical Staff of College Hospital, Cerritos, California and College Hospital Costa Mesa, Costa Mesa, California. He is also a Program Consultant for the Youth Response Unit at both hospitals.

Mr. Buntman has specialized in helping parents of problem teens for almost 20 years — and has helped tens of thousands of parents solve their teenager's problems.

Throughout the year, the Center for Family Life Enrichment, Inc. sponsors a series of lectures in Southern California at which Mr. Buntman speaks. The Center also produces and distributes copies of Mr. Buntman's cassette series on "How To Live With Your Teenager".

The Center for Family Life Enrichment has a staff which includes Psychiatrists, Psychologists, Licensed Clinical Social Workers, Marriage, Family and Child Counselors, and Educators who specialize in working with problem teens.

Acknowledgements

Many people helped with this book.

Ilene Saltzman Tilton, MFCC, took all of the data and organized it so that it could be presented in a way that would be helpful to parents.

Dr. Robert Davison, Glenda Davison, M.A., Dr. Johanna Fisher, Dr. Robert Leark, Denise Skovseth, LCSW, and Ilene Saltzman Tilton, MFCC, each spent time giving feedback, clarifying and adding to the book.

Mary Ellen Takayama researched and worked on the drafting and writing of Chapter 15.

Maureen Babbitt and Susan Ware did the extremely difficult task of proofreading the book.

Jill Voorhis of Extra! Extra! Graphics, St. Petersburg, Florida, diligently did the typesetting for draft after draft of this book.

Kare and Charles Possick contributed the cover design, graphic arts, layout and styling of the book.

Table of Contents

THEME ONE:
What You Need to Know About Your Teenager

Foreword 11
Introduction 13
Chapter 1 – Age-Appropriate Behavior 15
Chapter 2 – Friends 27
Chapter 3 – Communication 33
Chapter 4 – Peer Pressure 43
Chapter 5 – Allowances 47
Chapter 6 – Sibling Rivalry 51
Chapter 7 – Teenage Music 55
Chapter 8 – Anger 57
Chapter 9 – Compliments 59

THEME TWO:
How To Make Sure Your Teenager Doesn't Get Into Trouble

Chapter 10 – Jobs, Activities, Sports 61
Chapter 11 – Contracts 67
Chapter 12 – Discipline and Punishment 71

Chapter 13 – Limits and Setting Limits 81
Chapter 14 – Trust 89
Chapter 15 – Inpatient Treatment 91
Chapter 16 – Responsibility 101
Chapter 17 - Sex 103

THEME THREE:
What To Do If You're Having Lots Of Problems With Your Teen

Chapter 18 – Rebellion 107
Chapter 19 – School and School Problems 113
Chapter 20 – Drugs and Alcohol 123
Chapter 21 – Unacceptable Behavior 135
Chapter 22 – Out of Control 137
Chapter 23 – Running Away 143
Chapter 24 – When to Take Your Teen to Counseling 145

THEME FOUR:
Special Family Issues Involving Teenagers

Chapter 25 – Parenting 159
Chapter 26 – Divorce 161
Chapter 27 – Stepparenting 163
Chapter 28 – Single Parents 169
Chapter 29 – Eighteen On Up 173

Dedication

To Karla, my wife with whom I remain as eternally smitten as the first day.

— *Foreword* —
An Epidemic in Adolescence

We face an epidemic in dealing with our adolescents. Look at these statistics:

- Last year we had over 3.3 million adolescents who were alcoholics or had serious alcohol problems.
- Last year we had over 2.7 million adolescents who were drug addicts or had serious drug problems.
- Last year over 1.3 million adolescent girls became pregnant.
- Last year over 600,000 adolescents tried to kill themselves.
- Last year the second leading cause of death during adolescence was suicide.
- Last year, in a survey done by the National Institute of Health, 38% of all tenth-graders questioned said that they had had five or more alcoholic drinks on a single drinking occasion within the two weeks before the survey.
- The same survey also noted that about one-third of the teenagers who responded had "seriously thought" about suicide. About 20% of the girls, and 10% of the boys, had actually tried to take their own lives.

The goal of our philosophy is to help you live with your adolescent as amicably and harmoniously as possible.

The heart and soul of our philosophy is that parents need to be strict; they need to be firm; they need to set limits; and they need to keep to their limits.

This book is for parents who have serious problems with their adolescents; for parents who have any kind of problems with their adolescents; and for those who wish to prevent problems with their adolescents.

This book has specific and detailed answers for your questions. After you have read this book, I want you to have answers that you can put into practice immediately. This book, *How to Live with Your Teenager II: A Question and Answer Guide for Parents*, is the second of a two-book series. The first book, *How to Live with Your Teenager; a Survivor's Handbook for Parents,* teaches communication skills and specific ways to help you with your teenager. The book is specific, detailed and practical. To get the best use of this book it is imperative to have the first book. If you would like to order *How to Live with Your Teenager; a Survivor's Handbook for Parents,* please refer to Page 176 for information on how to obtain the first book.

Peter H. Buntman, M.S.W., ACSW
Licensed Clinical Social Worker
Director, Center for Family Life Enrichment, Inc.

Introduction

Between 35% and 40% of the families we meet at our Center for Family Life Enrichment have teenagers who are out of control. Your teenager is out of control if:
- he doesn't obey your curfew
- he leaves the house after you've told him to stay
- he abuses his parents
- he abuses his siblings
- he refuses to do chores
- he is not working up to grade level in each and every one of his school subjects
- he gets in trouble with his teacher at school
- he cuts school
- he doesn't go to school at all
- he uses drugs
- he uses alcohol
- he abuses food (he's twenty pounds or more overweight)
- he uses cigarettes
- he runs away
- he gets into trouble with the police and the law

This book, *How to Live with Your Teenager II: A Question and Answer Guide for Parents*, offers suggestions on how to get your adolescent back into control if he is out of control. The book also offers suggestions for parents whose teenagers are just starting to get out of control, as well as for parents who want to prevent their teenager from getting out of control.

This is the second book in a two-part series. The first book in the series, *How to Live with Your Teenager; a Survivor's Handbook for Parents*, is a "course in parenting" that includes a specific step-by-step plan that teaches parents concrete communication skills. By using a unique journal-in-the-book approach, the "course" helps parents put these communication skills into practice.

To maximize the effectiveness of this second book, you need to also read *How to Live with Your Teenager; a Survivor's Handbook for Parents*. You can order the first book on Page 176 of this one.

How to Live with Your Teenager; a Survivor's Handbook for Parents has sold over 100,000 copies, and is one of the all-time bestsellers among books about adolescence. It is nationally noted, and offers real help for parents.

The Center for Family Life Enrichment, Inc., specializes in helping the nine to nineteen-year-old age range, in short-term, individual, family and group counseling. We have offices throughout Orange County and parts of Los Angeles County, in the cities of Anaheim, Cerritos, Costa Mesa, Downey, Fullerton, Huntington Beach, Irvine, Lakewood, Los Alamitos, Orange, Torrance and Whittier. We offer short-term counseling designed to bring out-of-control teenagers back into control quickly. You can reach us at the Center at (213) 596-8712 or (714) 761-0844.

Between 40% and 45% of the families who have been to our Center have tried other types of therapy and counseling — none of which have worked. When parents have tried other counseling and it hasn't worked, they feel discouraged. They've invested a lot of time, effort, energy and money — without success. If your adolescent is out of control, or if he needs help, we urge you to call us to set up a time to come in for a free evaluation. An evaluation consists only of us sitting down and talking with you. Because our counseling specializes in working with nothing but adolescents and their families, we offer short-term, effective therapy in helping you get your adolescent back in control.

Ed Bloch, M.S.W.
Executive Director
Center for Family Life Enrichment, Inc.

> THEME ONE:
> What You Need To Know About Your Teenager

CHAPTER ONE

Age-Appropriate Behavior

Many parents do not know what age-appropriate behaviors are for an adolescent. Some parents are not aware that there are great differences between age-appropriate behaviors for a teen and age-appropriate behaviors for a child. The differences are quite surprising and sometimes shocking to parents.

A. Not Confiding

One facet of adolescence which seems to shock parents is that their teen, who as a child often confided in them, now rarely wants to talk to them at all—about anything. This is age-appropriate behavior for the adolescent.

Very often adolescents don't know how they feel. They are experiencing feelings that are totally new to them, and they can't even begin to put these feelings into words. They feel embarrassed and confused because they can't express these feelings. They don't understand them, and they don't want to admit this to their parents.

Teens also have many thoughts and opinions that they know their parents will not agree with. These thoughts and opinions may fall within the areas of drugs, sex, racial biases, religion, etc. Because of any of these reasons, they no longer confide or share things with them.

Parents sometimes react very strongly when their teens do not confide in them, and believe they have failed as parents. They feel upset because they don't know why their youngster stopped confiding in them. Parents of teens need to realize that not confiding in them, not talking over their problems with them, not discussing their feelings and ideas with them, is age-appropriate behavior.

Allowing your teens the space they need to be themselves, not pushing them, and yet at the same time letting them know that you're there when they need you, is the delicate balancing act parents of teens need to maintain.

B. Mood Swings

Drastic, lightning-quick changes of feelings and moods are totally age-appropriate for the adolescent. This is normal and natural teen behavior, and while parents find it irritating, exasperating and difficult to live with, it may help to realize that "this too, shall pass."

Teenagers sulk, get angry, are crabby, are irrational, are furious, are seething, are loving, are generous, are warm, are giving, are tolerant, and are understanding. Also, all these feelings (and others) switch back and forth very quickly.

C. A Teen's Need Not to Be With the Family

When children become teenagers they need time to be alone, time to be and talk with their friends, and time to participate in outside activities. All of this time adds up to periods away from the family. The teenager needs to become a person separate from the family, to begin to discover who he is and who he wants to be as a person. This process of separating spans several years and is a necessary, normal, and natural part of the teenager's development. In terms of behavior, they may not want to spend very much, if any, time with their family. They may refuse to go with the family when the family goes out; they may not want to spend holidays with their family; they may not even want to eat with the family very often. They simply want to separate, to have time away from their family.

Parents have a difficult time accepting this kind of behavior. Suddenly, their delightful youngster, who wanted to spend a lot of time with them, who was nice to have around, who was a joy to relate to, now has become a moody, surly, rebellious teenager who seems to reject them and resists being with them. When this happens, parents frequently take this rejection personally and demand that their teen spend more time with them. Fights start over this issue, communication stops, and everyone is unhappy.

When youngsters become teens, their need to spend time with the family may decline at an accelerated rate. As a parent of a teenager, when this happens, try to understand and accept his or her need to be away from you.

Teenagers are not children, they are adolescents. Teenagers don't need their parents in the same way they did when they were children. This is one of the greatest challenges parents of teenagers have to face—their teens need them differently now, and parents have to respond to that difference.

Invite your teen to go out with the family to dinner or to a movie. Invite her or him to be a part of all family outings. Teens need to know that they are welcome to join in all family activities. On the other hand, the parents need to understand and accept the fact that their teen needs to be alone and away from them at times, and very often will not join family activities.

One word of caution here: as a parent, you need to work very hard *not* to make your teen feel guilty about the need to be alone and away from you. Otherwise, your teen will feel that it's not all right to accept all his or her feelings.

D. Need to Rebel

Teenagers need to rebel or to reject, or to try on different ideas and values. This is their way of defining themselves. It is a natural and normal part of adolescence to rebel against the values and beliefs of parents and of society.

This means they are trying to define their own values and beliefs separate from yours. They may conclude this process by thinking and believing similarly or dissimilarly from you. But the point is that the values and beliefs will feel more "theirs" if they can complete this process.

Think back to when you were a teenager. Did you hold the same values as your parents? Were you in perfect agreement with your parents? Probably not. Did you lie? Did you cheat? Did you steal? Did you do things "behind your parents' back?" Probably yes.

Teenagers who are "goody-goody" (and not many of them truly are) are those who always listen to their parents and never get into trouble—in other words, "perfect" kids. "Perfect" kids don't rebel at all—but, almost always, those "perfect" teens will experience problems as an adult because they did not meet that mandatory growth requirement during adolescence, which is to *rebel*, to try on different values and beliefs, to define themselves.

There are many non-harmful ways for teens to rebel or define themselves, such as choice of music, sound level of music, hair style, messy room, sleeping late, clothes, jewelry, beliefs, etc. And, while it is not necessary for parents to like any of the non-harmful ways their teens choose to rebel, it is imperative to remember that the teen is fulfilling a psychological need when he or she does rebel.

Before you do battle over your teen's style of hair and loud music, make sure he or she has other non-harmful ways of rebelling. Otherwise, you may win the battle but lose the war when he or she chooses to rebel in a way you find totally unacceptable.

E. Peer Group Pressure

Another psychological need crucial to the adolescent is the need for peer group acceptance.

As adolescents rebel against society and parental values, they seek acceptance and support from their peer group. The less acceptance and support that teens get at home, either from parents or older family members, the more they will seek this from their peer group. However, no matter how much acceptance and support they get at home, they will still seek acceptance and approval from their peer group. During adolescence, the peer group influence is at its greatest, and often, if adolescents are forced to make a choice, they will choose the peer group's values rather than parental values.

Questions:

1. My daughter doesn't want to spend any time with me. All she wants to do is spend time with her friends. What can I do?

The first step is to be aware she is acting age-appropriately. The peer group has a greater influence at this age than any other time in a person's life.

What is most important is to maintain your relationship with her and leave open lines of communication. If there is a secret for relating to teenagers, it is to do things they like to do. You might offer to take her shopping when she needs clothes or school things. You can also invite her out for a Coke or something at McDonald's, since most teens like to eat.

2. My teenagers spend hours on end playing Nintendo video games. Is this all right?

Nintendo can be a very safe form of rebellion and an age-appropriate activity. Certainly kids cannot get into trouble by watching and playing video games. It is also a more common behavior for boys. If your adolescents are doing well in school and doing their chores and spending some time with their parents, then I do not see any problem letting them spend a fair amount of time playing Nintendo. On the other hand, if they are refusing to do chores and not doing well in school, I would severely limit the Nintendo until those other areas of their lives improve.

3. What can I do when my thirteen-year-old girl refuses to have anything to do with me or her father?

Again, you need to figure out what interests a thirteen-year-old girl. For example, the next time she needs school clothes, offer to take her shopping. If she needs something for school like a special notebook or colored paper, offer to take her. If she wants a CD or tape, offer to go to the record or tape store with her.

Then offer to take her for a Coke or a hamburger on the way to or from shopping. Another thing you might try is to ask her to a movie and let her choose it; then afterwards, ask her out for a Coke and talk about the movie.

4. What if I have tried all the suggestions mentioned and my teenager still refuses to do anything with me?

The first thing you need to look at is what you say to your daughter when you are alone with her. Closely examine the content of the conversation. You may find that you give too much advice because you do not get to see her very often. In the little time you have together, you may be trying to remind her what she needs to do better, what she had neglected to do during the week, or what mistakes you have made which she should avoid. Many parents give their children a lot of tips they think will be appreciated so that the children will not have to learn the hard way. Often, the kids do not seem to listen and the parents just keep repeating themselves.

Teenagers tell me that when they spend time with their parents, the parents give them lectures, repeat things again and again, constantly criticize and ask a whole bunch of questions the kids do not want to talk about. Your relationship with your daughter seems to be fairly distant at this point. What I think you need to say to yourself is, "I am not going to lecture, criticize or give advice to my daughter when we go out, but have a good time with her and talk about the things in which she is interested."

Even if she slurps her Coke at McDonald's, that is not the time to bring it up. When you are out with your daughter, resort to "small talk" for lack of anything else. For example, talk about whether you should have a fish sandwich or a double cheeseburger, about which recordings she is going to buy, what she likes about a particular rock group, and things like that. It is also important to give praise and compliments.

If you can create a climate where there is quality time for her as well as you, she will want to do more.

5. My fifteen-year-old son goes directly to his room when he comes home from school, gets some snacks later from the kitchen and goes back to his room, but will never eat with us. Is this normal?

Yes, it is normal and natural for adolescents to want to be alone and not spend time with their parents. But the degree to which he is avoiding you is not appropriate. Often parents have given up control in one or many areas of their children's lives. They need to regain control. I suggest you tell your son, "We understand you want to be alone. That is fine. However, we are going to insist you eat dinner with us every evening. You do not have a choice, and will have to be with us during dinner." You also might add, "We want you to be around us an hour in the evening, but do not care what you do, even if it's just watching TV. Come and spend at least an hour in the evening with us."

6. How much phone time should an adolescent have?

It depends on a number of things; how many phone lines are in the house, and how well they are doing in school and around the house. Wanting to use the phone continually is a very age-appropriate behavior for adolescents, so if they are doing well in school, working up to their ability, doing their chores and there are enough phone lines in the house, it is fine to let them use the phone as much as they want (which may appear to you as all the time). If teenagers are not doing well in school, not working up to their ability, have not done their chores, or there is only one phone in the house, then you need to limit the phone in some way.

7. My daughter has a terribly messy room. Clothes are everywhere and she knows how much I hate it. The only thing which seems to work in getting her to change is taking away horseback riding. She loves her horse and takes care of it meticulously. Yet if I take away the TV or anything else, she does not care.

Having a messy room is an extremely safe way to rebel. It seems her horseback riding is part of an overall responsibility which has probably been very good for her self-esteem. She probably goes to the stable every day, feeds the horse, cleans up after it and exercises it. To take that away from her would be like taking away a child's participation in a sport which is very good for building self-esteem. I see the horseback riding as an extremely positive activity which also teaches her a form of responsibility.

Personally, I could live with the messy room. But, if you cannot, you might try giving her extra chores, taking away some part of her allowance or making her go to bed early.

8. Is it age-appropriate behavior for a younger adolescent to insist on eating only three items?

I suggest talking to your family doctor about it since this might also be a medical question.

9. Is lying an age-appropriate behavior?

Almost all adolescents lie sometimes. However, whether it is age-appropriate or not depends on the degree. If teenagers lie now and then, you need to call them on it when you catch it and tell them it is not acceptable. Such occurrences are in the normal range of behavior. But, if your teens are chronic liars, it is a serious problem. If you catch them red-handed and they will not admit it, if they rationalize things all the time (always blame someone else for their problems or difficulties), if they lie about issues which are important such as whether or not they go to school, use drugs or cut classes, it is a severe problem. There are a number of things you can do if your teen lies. Each one needs to be applied to the situation carefully with your own judgment. One thing is to say, "Look, I am going to make a deal with you, lying is not acceptable. I will ask you a question and you have two choices. One is to tell me the truth and the other is to say nothing, but do not lie."

Or you could say, "Whatever answer you give me, I will not punish you." But, be prepared to hear things you may dislike, and resist your desire to punish the kid if you ever want him or her to tell you the truth again.

Adolescents who are chronic liars have a serious problem and need counseling.

10. What can I do about an argumentative teenager? She questions everything and won't drop a subject.

Argumentation is a safe form of rebellion and is age-appropriate. The question really is how to handle it. If she argues about things like taking a shower when she obviously knows she needs to take a shower, this is just a safe way to rebel. The issue becomes how you handle it. One way is simply to tell her your reason and walk away from the argument. If she follows and tries to continue, punish her. There is no rule that a parent has to listen to arguments.

If you are patient enough, you might want to listen a little longer. However, if you are not in the mood to listen, set your limit and stick to it.

11. What if your twelve-year-old daughter wants to go out with a seventeen-year-old boy on a date and she says all her friends are doing it?

It is probably not true that her friends are doing it, but is age-appropriate for a twelve-year-old girl to want to date older boys. Yet, it would be very inappropriate to allow such behavior. I would tell the twelve-year-old, "Hey, you cannot date until you are at least fifteen or sixteen." You should not even allow her to talk on the phone to a seventeen-year-old boy. Then explain to her why a seventeen-year-old boy would be interested in a twelve-year-old girl, and forbid her to see the seventeen-year-old boy.

12. How do I get my son to cut his long hair? It drives my husband up the wall, and I do not particularly like it either.

If your son is doing reasonably well in school, working up to his grade potential, does reasonably well at home, does chores, is not into alcohol or drugs, and has decent friends, yet wants to wear his hair long or maybe even to have an earring, I would thank a Higher Power. He is rebelling in a way which may be turning your stomach into a knot, but it is at least safe. Be thankful he is not rebelling with drugs or alcohol.

13. My teenager always needs to be reminded to do her chores. It is an ongoing struggle to get her to do them. How long should she be allowed to continue getting away with this?

Continually refusing to do chores or having to be reminded is a safe form of rebellion which is age-appropriate. It may not even be a case of forgetfulness, but of her testing you, which is also common during adolescence.

By testing, I mean challenging your rules and what you say. The challenge may come directly or indirectly where she refuses to do things or seemingly forgets.

The testing, whether it is direct or indirect, almost always drives a parent up a wall, which is what teenagers try to do subconsciously with their rebelling. What you can do with chores is set your limit, then go ahead and punish infractions. Again, it will be a perpetual process of testing and restricting. Perservering in controlling the testing will result in her respecting you in the long run. However, do not clamp down too hard on this safe form of rebellion and cause her to rebel in unsafe ways.

14. How do I know whether I am overreacting, or my teen's behavior truly is wrong and inappropriate? So many of the things you suggest are confusing to me because I do not know if my teenager's behavior falls in the age-appropriate or an unsafe range.

That is a thoughtful question. Sometimes it is very difficult to separate the issues. Parenting has become so much more complicated in the last decades of this century. What I urge parents to do is go to a counselor for an annual checkup, just as you would go to a dentist or doctor once or twice a year. Raising a teenager healthily is hard enough to do without any outside opinions or advice. Especially if you are ever in doubt, go to a professional for a checkup.

15. Is punk hair an acceptable form of rebellion?

It depends what is going on in the other parts of the adolescent's life. I have rarely seen punk hair without their involvement with the whole punk scene, which includes listening to punk or heavy metal music full of lyrics describing devil worship, Satan, and sexual perversions. Invariably, when teens are involved in this behavior, their grades begin to decline, and drug and/or alcohol use follows. Such behavior is mentally and physically unhealthy and calls for immediate counseling.

16. You give us all these different guidelines for teenagers, but how can we really know if our teenager is displaying safe adolescent behavior when teenagers are so different?

Here is the way I judge whether a teenager is doing relatively well. If she or he is working up to capacity in school, gets along reasonably well at home, does their chores, has decent friends and obeys your rules and regulations fairly well, then he or she is doing fine.

17. I am a working mother of three, and my oldest boy of sixteen does not cooperate very much with me. I get sick of doing things for him, like his laundry and picking up after him, but I worry that if I stop, he will not take care of himself.

There is no reason your sixteen-year-old cannot do his own laundry. Tell him you are not going to do it anymore, you do not appreciate his lack of cooperation, and he is responsible for doing his own laundry and cleaning up. If he does not have any clean clothes, that is his problem. You can enforce his not cleaning up and not doing chores.

18. My teenager is always testing me. She interprets every rule her own way—she keeps stretching them and breaking them. It seems as if I were at battle with her all the time. Is this normal?

Absolutely. I mentioned earlier that a normal age-appropriate behavior is testing. For example, just after you have reached an agreement that no friends will be entertained in the house, she might bring someone over and say that she is like her sister and not really a friend. Go ahead and punish her. The testing and pushing may never seem to end. It is demanding, relentless, unyielding, and it is an age-appropriate characteristic of teenagers. Just follow through with punishments and hold out.

19. Our son seems so perfect. He never gets into trouble or rebels and we are concerned. As you said earlier, teenagers like that have a bad time later on. What can we do?

You can help him feel that making mistakes or not being perfect is all right. So, when he does something which is not perfect, like being a few minutes late doing chores, do not criticize him but give him space to make errors.

The dynamics behind the adolescent who is a perfectionist is usually the unconscious process of rationalizing that "no one will criticize me if I am perfect, so if I do not want to be criticized, I must be perfect." This stems from insecurities deep inside a person. One way to work on this is to give your teen a lot of compliments and praise, and let him or her know it is all right not to have everything one-hundred percent perfect all the time.

20. My thirteen-year-old girl is starting to dress differently. I think she looks awful. She is wearing more eye makeup than I want, she wears green and black all the time and wraps her hair up. What do I do?

I think wearing green and black is a personal preference, and it is a safe form of rebellion as well as wearing her hair up. If you want to set a limit about how much eye makeup she can wear, go ahead and do it; the other two are just safe forms of rebellion.

21. I am worried about my fifteen-year-old girl who fantasizes about being married to a movie star.

Again, it is a matter of degree. It is common for girls to fantasize about being married to movie or rock stars. It is also common for boys to fantasize about being rock stars, football, or baseball players. The concern I would have is whether it is out of balance. If the girl spends all of her time in her room staring at a poster of a rock or movie star and seems obsessed, then there is a problem. If she just collects his CDs, videos or movies, and talks about him a lot, then it is age-appropriate behavior.

22. Is it age-appropriate behavior if siblings do not speak to each other or recognize they are in the house?

It is an extreme, but yes, it is probably age-appropriate.

23. My twelve-year-old daughter and I spend all our time together, yet, recently, she chose to read a book instead of spending time with me, and I feel really hurt.

Part of what happens as a child enters adolescence is to spend less time with parents and more time alone. It is age-appropriate, and it is important for you to realize that while you can invite your teen out, she may not want to go with you as much now that she becomes more independent.

24. What do you do with a teenager who sulks when you set a limit?

Ignore him and let him sulk. You might say, "If you want to sulk, that is OK, but go to your room and do it."

25. Our fourteen-year-old daughter wants to go with her girlfriends to a roller skating rink, be dropped off and picked up later. But there are a lot of boys at the rink who are much older and use drugs. What should I do?

Tell her it is not appropriate for her to be there. Do not let her go. See if there is another time, like in the afternoon, when the boys do not hang out there. Then, if she really wants to go roller skating, bring her and then stay and watch for a while.

26. How do you reconcile your policy of being strict with teenagers and their need to rebel?

You formulate a strategy where you let your teenager rebel in safe ways, while you are strict about things which concern their health, safety, and welfare. An example of safe rebellion is having clothes all over the room: this doesn't hurt your teen, while rebelling with drugs does. You know they are going to rebel, push and test; but if you can give them enough space while still maintaining limits, you are acting as a responsible parent.

CHAPTER TWO

Friends

During adolescence, the peer group has strong influence. Adults and parents in particular often have little rapport with the teen during these years. This does not mean that you cannot override bad peer influence on your teen, since this is one of your jobs as a parent. If your teenager has few friends, or does not have any friends, this chapter will give suggestions on what to do and how to help that situation.

It is extremely rare that a teenager who has very few friends or no friends at all, doesn't yearn for more friends. Having few or no friends often is an indication of a terrible unhappiness. These are problems parents should not ignore. The other major question that parents have concerning friends is what to do about friends you think are harmful to your teen. This chapter also addresses that issue.

Questions:

1. What reason can I give my twelve-year-old daughter for not wanting her to go to the mall alone with her friends unsupervised?

It depends on how much you trust your daughter. If you trust her sufficiently you could say to her, "We will take you to the mall or beach with your friends and leave you there for a few hours and then pick you up at such-and-such time." If you do not trust her, tell her the reasons why you will not let her go alone. Then you could tell her what she needs to do to regain your trust. About the mall; if you feel uncomfortable letting her go there because of the possibility of drinking or other things about which you are unhappy, you could tell her why. For example, "It doesn't feel right

Friends 27

to me for these reasons, and you cannot do that until you are this age."

2. My fifteen-year-old son in high school wants to make friends, but does not feel he is fitting in. He doesn't have any friends and doesn't know what to do.

One thing you could do is to encourage him to invite friends over to the house. You could say, "Look, I know it is hard, but why don't you invite this kid over, and while he is here, I will go with the two of you and we will rent a movie for the VCR." Encourage him to take the initiative in making friends.

You could also encourage him to join activities such as church or synagogue, youth groups, school activities or activities from the city's recreation department. Through such contacts, he will become more comfortable with peers and make friends easier with greater confidence.

You might even role-play with him and ask him to pretend you are a friend and he is going to ask you over.

Making friends with other kids involves a series of relatively complicated skills. Most kids learn this intuitively. These skills often are quite specific, since the way one asks someone over can either turn a kid off or entice him to come.

3. My son likes having his friends over all the time, but my husband objects because when he comes home from work, he is tired and cannot stand the constant noise. My son also wants to bring his friends on vacation. However, my husband says the noise and music irritates him.

What you might do is suggest to your husband that having friends over is really great because then you know where your son is and he can't possibly get into trouble while being supervised. Your husband also has a right to a certain amount of time a week alone without the kids. You or your husband could explain this to your son. Another thing you might tell your son is, "There are certain times when dad needs to have it quiet, so why don't you go to this part of the house and not make any noise, so that dad will let you have your friends over more often."

I think it is great if a kid is allowed to take a friend on vacation. This could even help, because while you are relaxing by the pool at a motel, reading a magazine, the kids could be entertaining each other away from you in the pool and not bothering you. In another setting, they could be entertaining each other rather than being with you and getting on your nerves. I would suggest you give it a

28 How to Live with Your Teenager II

whirl with your husband to see if you can sell him on the advantage of having your son with his friend on vacation.

4. We have two teenage sons and all their friends are here all the time. We go into the bedroom to give them freedom in the house because we have a small house; but we are tired of living our lives in the bedroom after dinner and on weekends. I do not want to tell his friends that they cannot come over, though.

The advantage of this situation is that if your son's friends are at your home, they cannot get into trouble under close supervision, which is great. It is also a compliment to your son and you that they feel comfortable there.

On the other hand, you do not have to be prisoners in your bedroom. When you want to watch a TV program, you could come out to watch it and simply say to your sons, "We want to watch this program and you are welcome to join us." You have the right to use your house too, and, since it is small, you could put restrictions on how often and how long their friends can stay.

5. What can you do if your son or daughter is hanging around kids you do not like?

It depends on the age, how much you dislike them, and why you dislike them. If the kids are doing destructive things like taking alcohol, dope, or not going to school, you can say, "Hey, as of right now you are not to associate with that kid, period!" If you do that, make sure you can enforce it. See the chapter on kids who are out of control. The other thing you can do is to take the subtle approach, encouraging your teenager to have other friends who you consider better for your son or daughter. You might say, "Why not invite this kid to the house," or, "I would be glad to take you and this friend to a movie." This will make your teen less defensive. The tactic of trying to stop your adolescent from being with another kid will sometimes drive them closer together; but I do not think you have a choice if the friend is distructive in the ways I've indicated.

6. Do you have any suggestions for a teenage boy who is too shy, does not want to take any risks to meet people, will not reach out in any way, yet does not appear to be very unhappy?

Such behavior tells you something is wrong, since you know he goes to school, sees a whole bunch of guys talking about going to a movie, a ball game or surfing, and he knows he is different. He needs to learn these social skills for life. Whereas most kids learn these automatically, others need to learn them in other ways. It can be very difficult making friends since so much is involved in the process. For example, to have a relationship you must introduce yourself to someone, then after you say "Hi!" you have to say something else. If you want to ask another kid to come over to your house, you say, "Hey, do you want to come over?" Then you must figure out what to do once he gets there.

What we do at our Center with adolescents lacking social skills is to use group therapy to teach them the skills of being in relationships. These are social skill classes which are not as much therapy as they are lessons in the specific skills needed to help build an adolescent's confidence.

7. Our teenage son is really shy. He rarely sees other kids and refuses to have them over to our house despite the fact we ask them and have things kids would enjoy, such as a pool table and VCR.

There is usually a specific reason for behavior which your son displays. First, he may not know how to ask kids over. Second, he may be afraid he will be rejected. Third, he may think that something you and your husband are doing may be embarrassing to him; for example, the way your husband dresses, or the color of your living room drapes, or the fact he does not have a certain amount of privacy. I suggest that you talk to him to see if anything in your house (by his perception and in his mind) is causing him not to invite friends over.

8. My fifteen-year-old son has only one friend who is twenty-one. This friend does not go to school or work, and I suspect he is using alcohol and drugs. What should I do?

I am concerned about a twenty-one-year-old who does not go to school or work, and may be using alcohol and drugs. He would certainly be a bad influence on your son. I would also question the motivation of the twenty-one-year-old to hang around a fifteen-year-old kid. He must be pretty immature. But I am even more concerned about your suspicion of his drug and alcohol use.

If it is more than a suspicion, you should tell your son not to hang around this twenty-one-year-old because of the drugs and alcohol and encourage him, through all the things I have suggested in this chapter, to make other friends.

9. How do I keep my teenager, who is a good kid, from hanging around those I know are bad?

It depends on the age, but if you feel strongly that these kids are a bad influence on your child, you could say, "Look, you are not going to run around with these kids and here is why." Then, do whatever you must to enforce it.

CHAPTER THREE

Communication

There are many reasons, on both sides of the adolescent-parent relationship, why communication is so difficult. It is during these years your teenager begins to strive for independence, which means trying to form a life and identity exclusive from yours. Parents wonder why their teenagers share less of their feelings and lives with them, not realizing this is a process adolescents must go through. While going through this, adolescents often do not know how they feel, which makes it hard for them to verbalize their feelings to you, even if they wanted to.

> *On the other side, many times parents lack real listening skills. They hear the words their teen is saying but not the meaning. Parents are sometimes so full of advice that they dismiss their son or daughter's opinion. This only leads to resentment, which will cause your teen not to approach you next time. It is age-appropriate for your teenager to speak with you less, and this may worry you, make you feel hurt, or even angry. However, you need to keep the doors of communication open for your teenager's sake. Your feelings are all right to have, but do not let them get in the way of hearing your teenager. Instead, develop your listening skills.*

Keeping their thoughts to themselves gives teenagers a sense of privacy and self-identity which a parent needs to respect, so long as it does not conflict with parental responsibility. Yet, there are things you have to talk to your teen about no matter what. Using your listening skills as the "I" message and "You're feeling" message (as I outlined in *How To Live With Your Teenager A Survivor's Handbook For Parents*) will open communication and help you decipher a complicated language called teenagese.

Things which will ease the process of communicating even more during the adolescent years are, for example, trying to see your teenager's point of view, being open to new ideas, letting your teenager make his or her own decisions (as long as they are fairly reasonable and safe), and most important, using your listening skills. These are hard things to do, but it is worse if your teen gets into trouble because he or she cannot talk to you because of feeling that you do not listen and do not value his or her opinion.

Questions:

1. What can I do if my teenager refuses to talk to me? When I ask how are things, he says "Fine"; when I ask about his day he says "OK"; and whenever I try to see what he wants to talk about, he says "Nothing."

Sometimes when I ask adults and parents what they mean by communicating with their adolescent, they mean sharing each other's day and talking about things of interest to both of them. Teenagers are extremely selfish. They are basically uninterested in us as parents, our lives, our work, our TV programs or what goes on with their relatives. They are mostly oblivious to adults in general, and parents in particular. They are entirely absorbed in their own world. So, if there is a secret for communicating with teenagers, it is talking to them about their own lives, friends, music, activities at school and things of interest to them. Essentially, the nature of the adult/teenager relationship is one of 99% giving on the part of the adult, and 99% taking on the part of the teenager.

2. What happens if you try to talk to them at their level about their music, friends and other self-interests, and they still refuse to communicate?

You are not alone. In approximately 30% to 40% of families, there is little or no communication. My suggestion is to start with things in which they are obviously interested. For example, I would sit down and watch a TV program your teenager is watching. At the end of the program you might try asking what she or he thought, or, at least, say what you thought. You start in a very safe area in order to develop the basis for communication. Afterwards, when you have a comfortable level built up, you could talk about other things. But, it will take time. In the proccess it is important to use your attentive listening skills.

3. What else can I do to begin communicating with my teenager? We have not really talked about anything in three years. All he ever says is "yes," "no," "OK."

I would start by trying to make a list of things your teen is interested in, and then get involved. For example, if he is an eleven-year-old who likes to play video games, go play video games with him; if he is a fourteen-year-old boy who likes fishing, then do that with him; or if she is a thirteen-year-old girl who likes to go shopping, go to the mall with her. Again, the secret to relating with teenagers is to do things in which they are interested, and to bear with the age-appropriate selfishness of their behavior. Have them rent a movie for your VCR one night. By watching the movie they have chosen, you have more of a common interest with them. Or, you might try inviting them to a theater for a movie of their choice. Most of the movies these days seem to be geared for kids thirteen-to-twenty-years old, so there will most likely be something playing that interests them. Following the movie, you could go out for a hamburger and soda (most teenagers enjoy eating), and discuss what you saw. Rebuilding the relationship like this, and using your attentive listening skills to show that you care, will make it easier for your teenager to talk to you and share more. You must start some place, and the key is to discover their own interests. So, find out what your teenagers' hobbies are, and what they do with their time, and do it with them.

4. My teen does not have any interests or hobbies. What do I do then?

Most every teenager is interested in at least two things. One is watching TV or listening to music, and the other is eating. So begin with that. Slowly but surely, by watching a few programs together and going out for a snack once a week, your teen will open up to new things.

5. I am divorced and my son, who is nine, lives on the other side of the country in Florida with his mother. How can I have a relationship with him when I see him only at Christmas and for two weeks in the summer?

Do it by phone: find out what your nine-year-old watches on TV and watch the programs too. Find out if he goes to movies and what he likes. Then, you see the same movies and call him twice a week to talk about what you both saw. At that age, kids usually enjoy talking about those things. Then, you could work into other subjects. Also, you could write letters and cards telling him about a great TV program you saw, or asking what he thought of a certain movie.

6. What if your thirteen-year-old girl wants nothing to do with you and refuses all your invitations?

You need to figure out what interests a thirteen-year-old girl. A father once told me that he took his son fishing for three years, yet never took the time to figure out that his son hated fishing. The boy hated putting the worms on the hook, and the slimy fish. You then need to figure out activities your thirteen-year-old daughter will probably do with you. When she needs clothes, you might offer to take her. You may not even like shopping, but it is a place to start. After a day of shopping, you could stop for a soda to rest and talk about what colors she likes, what outfits go together, the latest fashions, etc. Or, perhaps, the next time she wants a CD or tape you could take her to the store, asking her on the way about her favorite group or singer.

7. How long will all this take? How many movies must I see? How many TV programs must I watch? And how much fast food must I eat?

It could take three or four months or longer if there has been no real communication over an extended period of time. Just imagine if you were a salesperson and needed to get an important customer who had refused you three or four times. Would you give up? Of course not. You would go after the customer and be persistent. And, once you got the contract, all your persistence will have paid off. How much more important is your own family? Few people have easy jobs or lives, and most work very hard. But I believe when you get home, your real job of parenting begins. So, one should work even harder at being the best parent possible.

While I cannot guarantee that your teenager will talk to you, I can tell you that these are strategies that do work for many people. After repeatedly asking your kids about the things in which they are interested, something will click in their heads. If you are not judgmental and use your attentive listening skills, they will feel it is safe to talk more and open up.

8. My fifteen-year-old daughter comes home from school, goes straight to her room and only comes out for dinner,

refusing to talk to me at all. What can I do?

First of all, tell her there are some new rules in the house. You might say, "I can understand that you want some privacy and time alone, but it is not good for you to spend all your time in your room. The first rule is that you must be out of your room for at least an hour and a half and eat dinner with the family. You don't have to talk to me an hour and a half; but you must be somewhere in this house, watching TV, studying or whatever, outside your room." More than likely she will watch TV or listen to music. Then, at least you could join your daughter watching TV or listening to music and have some basis for opening communication as discussed before.

9. *What else can I do to increase communications?*

Give a lot of praise. Building self-esteem is also an important part of communication. Give your kids at least three compliments a day.

10. *What if my teenager has inherited the ability to internalize feelings from his father. I can see the anger in his face, yet he will not talk about it or verbalize it?*

I do not believe one can inherit the ability to internalize feelings—it is not genetic but something which he learned. Children learn it from an adult or a role model. What I suggest is to go the other direction. When you watch TV or go to a movie together, you might say, "You look as if you really enjoyed the movie." Probably it will be less threatening for him to say "Yah, this guy killed this guy and these guys shot that one and it made me really happy." You want to start by helping him to identify and verbalize his positive feelings (such as being happy). When he has mastered this and can talk about what makes him feel good or happy, then he might start to acknowledge negative feelings. Furthermore, while discussing the movie over a hamburger or whatever, it is important to show him it is all right to acknowledge his feelings. You can do this by giving some praise, such as, "That was really neat you could share your feelings with me." Then he will feel more comfortable about acknowledging feelings in the future.

11. *How can I spend more time talking and doing things with my teenager when I am angry because she is doing things which you say are normal, like rebelling and being selfish? I become so angry that I do not even want to talk to her.*

What I suggest is that you realize the attitude you have is also normal and appropriate, since, when our teenagers are acting rebellious and selfish, it definitely makes us feel angry. Your acknowledgement of your own feelings is an important step toward happiness for you and your family. First of all, it helps you to identify your feelings so that you can deal with them constructively. Secondly, it gives your teenager a very good model to follow so that she will also learn how to deal with her anger in a positive way.

12. My son and I are constantly at war with each other, and despite the fact he is thirteen, it seems we are going to end up killing one another. During this "war" which has lasted the last two years, we have had no real communication.

This is an extreme case. I would not suggest doing this all the time, but when you come to the point of wanting to yell at him, stop and say, "Look, I feel really angry with you and I do not like being this way. So let's go out tonight to a movie, not because you have done something good, but because I want to spend some positive time with you. You and I need to do something we will both like, since the way things are going is just not good."

13. Why is it that whenever I discuss something negative with my daughter or criticize her in any way, she always blows up? She yells, screams, swears, and eventually storms out of the house and does not come back for hours.

It is all too common that the only communication many parents have in their families is negative, and as a result, the kid feels criticized. Take steps to improve your communication, including complimenting your teen, building up her self-esteem and "I" messages along with other positive forms of communication.

14. What can you do when your three children are upset because their natural father stops seeing them. He used to visit every other week but hasn't seen them for a year now?

You can encourage your kids to talk about it and to verbalize their feelings that they are hurt, angry, and upset. Depending on their ages, you might have them write their father asking him to visit or call them. Writing the letter or making the phone call may not get the results they desire, but at least it will help them to express their feelings, an important skill we all need to learn. They may also be feeling helpless since there is little they can do to get their father to see them. You can use attentive listening skills to help them understand their own feelings about the situation, but do not say anything negative about their father.

15. If I do not point out to my kids how bad my ex-husband is, that he is a sneak, a liar, and uncaring, how will they ever realize what a bad example he is?

If you want to get that across to the kids, in the long run you are using the worst strategy possible. Because, when you attack him, they will immediately want to come to his defense, even if they do not verbalize that to you. Children are a part of both parents, so when you attack the father you are attacking them.

16. Is it normal for a seventeen-year-old to get up and walk out of the room the minute I enter, even if he is watching TV, and does this mean he is on drugs?

No, it is not typical, but that does not necessarily mean he is on drugs. While I would not rule out the possibility of drugs, it may just be that he has not developed a better way of dealing with his feelings or anger. I would give him an "I" message sometime when you and he are alone. For example, "I really feel hurt when someone I love walks out of the room every time I enter, and won't even stay long enough to say "hello." If you are concerned about drugs, watch carefully for signs that might indicate it (see the chapter on drugs).

17. There are so many things that bug me about my teenager that I am always on her case. But, if I do not yell, she will continue to drive me crazy.

Almost every parent who has an adolescent could make a list of twenty things or more that bug them about their teenager. But if we are always getting on our kids' cases about things that bug us, then the only type of communication we are using with them is negative. What kids do with this kind of parent is to turn off and simply stop listening. My suggestion is to list about twenty things that bug you about your teenager, pick the top three to talk about, and ignore the rest. It really involves your making a decision to create a good or tolerable relationship with your kid now and a closer relationship in the long run. So, simply ignore most of the things which bother you now and concentrate only on three. For example, crucial things to talk about are not doing well in school, or hanging around peers who influence her negatively. While things like never cleaning her room or not doing chores can drive you nuts, they are not crucial areas on which to wage a major battle; they can be left alone. You certainly could feel free to mention it, but again, you want to concentrate on long term as well as short term relationships.

18. Is it a parent's responsibility to teach values?
Absolutely. One of the major ways children learn values is by watching their parents. Kids unconsciously uses the same sex parent as a role model and the opposite sex parent for their concept of men and women. If you want to talk to your adolescent about things like drugs or working up to their capacity in school, it is usually best to do the following: l. Pick a time when teenagers are not too busy and say that you want to talk. 2. Tell them that you are really concerned about this issue because you think it may be a problem for all teenagers, and you want to let them know how you feel about it, limiting your talk to about three or four minutes, otherwise, you will lose their attention. In order to keep their attention you could draw them into the discussion by asking questions about what they think about what you have said. Explore if they have any of their own questions. The better you communicate with your teenagers, the more you will be able to draw them out. If you have good communications and they ask questions, that is great. If not, just start with the lecture and after a while hopefully they will come to you with questions and talk more openly with you.

It is a mistake to lecture for fifteen minutes or to repeat yourself continually, thinking that this will make your teenager get it. If that kind of communication exists in your family, cut your lectures down to three or four minutes, since almost anything you would need to say can be said in that time.

19. What can I do if my adolescent refuses to visit her grandmother? The whole family goes every Sunday, but she says it is boring and won't go.
You might try some type of compromise. You could say, "Look, because you are a family member you have certain family reponsibilities, and one of them is seeing grandma. I know it is boring for you, so maybe we could work out a compromise so that you go every other time or every third time."

20. My teenager gets pretty good grades in school, but he does his homework with the TV on all the time. Wouldn't he do better if the TV were off? Whenever I shut it off, he throws a tantrum.

There is research that shows that some kids can concentrate extremely well with the TV or radio on; they just see it as a comfort or a soothing noise. They turn it on and concentrate on their homework. If your teen is doing well in school, leave it alone. If not, tell him that until he shows an improvement, the TV will remain off when he is doing homework.

21. My fifteen-year-old daughter told me that her best girlfriend is sexually active. What should I do about this—tell her friend's mother?

My guess is that your daughter is really asking what you think about her being sexually active and, how you would handle that. Here it is very appropriate for you to make a statement in a non-judgmental way, specifically how you feel. Many times kids throw out questions unconciously in order to test how you would respond if they followed that type of behavior. It is also important to emphasize that while you certainly do not approve of your daughter's being sexually active, if she ever were, you would hope that she would come to talk to you about venereal diseases and birth control. And, if she were to talk with you about this, it would not mean you approved, but that it is something which can be talked about.

I would not suggest you tell the friend's mother because it would be a violation of your daughter's privacy and confidentiality, and she would probably not trust you in the future to confide things of a personal and important nature.

22. What do I do as a single parent with three children when my oldest child monopolizes all of my attention, and at dinner, talks, and does not allow the other two to talk?

There is research that shows that the oldest child in an average family will monopolize 70% to 80% of the conversation. As a parent, you need to set limits and say, "I am really glad to hear about that, but I want to hear what Johnny and Susie did today, too." You do not want to turn your oldest one off, but give a clear message that you are interested in all of them. Another approach is to say, "The dinner table is for everyone to share. I am really happy you are sharing and you do it well. I hope Johnny and Susie can learn to share their feelings as well as you did. Now I would like to have the two of you share."

Then you need to be firm on setting limits with the oldest.

CHAPTER FOUR

Peer Pressure

Peer pressure is never stronger than during adolescence.

Questions:

1. What do you do if your fourteen-year-old teenager has friends you do not approve of?

It depends on why you do not approve of them. If they use drugs or alcohol, or are involved in criminal acts such as shoplifting or vandalism, or are cutting school, then you could tell your son, "This person is destructive because of this reason, and I am not going to allow you to be with him, period."

On the other hand, if you do not have any concrete reasons, and just dislike him because he has long hair or is a little bit rude to you, you should really evaluate whether you want to go to war on that issue.

Another thing is to subtly encourage your teen to be around friends of whom you approve. Suggest that he invite such a friend over to spend the night or to watch a movie on the VCR. Make it really convenient for him by picking this kid up, going with them to the video store and supplying refreshments. This is a very effective way of encouraging your son to be with kids you think are a good influence.

I caution you not to judge your son's friends just on looks, for sometimes a kid with long hair or an earring is displaying normal forms of rebellion, and could be an appropriate companion for your son. On the other hand, some really clean cut kids who are polite and charming may be very destructive. So do not be fooled by appearances.

2. What do you do with a fourteen-year-old girl who doesn't have a peer group, does not have any friends and does not do anything with kids her own age?

I would guess that this situation has existed for a while. Somewhere along the line, your daughter did not learn the social skills which most kids learn intuitively when they are younger.

There is a whole set of specific skills involved in making friends. They include things such as saying "hello," making conversation, asking questions, giving appropriate body language, knowing how to share, knowing how to participate with other kids in activities, learning to recognize when one does something which turn others off, learning how to act appropriately in different environments such as at another person's house, inviting kids over to your house, coming across in a way which makes others want to be your friend, etc.

My belief is that your daughter is not very happy since she sees others with friends and she is not included. Her problem is that she does not posess the skills needed for dealing with her peers for some reason or another.

The first thing you might do is to insist that she join some activity, whether it is an interest group at the park district such as karate or art, or a church or synagogue youth group, band, choir or a sport. Then, after she has an activity, you might encourage her to reach out and start making friends by asking someone over. Again, I would encourage you to make it very convenient for her by offering to pick the other kid up, taking them to a video store to rent a movie for the VCR, providing food and providing an atmosphere which is conducive to making friends.

We use group therapy at our Center to help adolescents like your daughter learn these social skills. While these kids often do not have additional psychiatric problems, they just do not have the skills to make friends. Group therapy becomes a living laboratory which helps them to learn and develop these skills.

3. We insist that our daughter get good grades since she is capable of getting all "A's." But she says if she gets good grades her friends tease her about being a brain and pick on her, and she wants to be popular.

What you might do is tell her to say to her friends, "Yes, grades are important to me and I am proud of what I get." Just say that without pushing it and see what happens. I would really question what kind of friends your daughter has if they tease her for getting good grades.

Another option, which I do not necessarily recommend but might work in your case, is to tell your daughter to blame it on you. She can say that her mother said she must get "A's" because that is what she is capable of, and if she does not, she will get in trouble and be grounded.

4. What can be done with a nine-year-old boy who is becoming so violent at school with his friends that he is expelled?

We are seeing more and more adolescent behaviors in children as young as ten and sometimes even younger. Adolescents often talk to us through their behavior. They are confused and do not have the verbal skills to tell us if they are unhappy or what problems they have.

When a boy becomes this angry and violent, he is telling us with his behavior that there is something wrong. He is saying, "I hurt inside and I need help."

He cannot be happy inside being violent toward his friends and getting expelled from school. This is clearly a situation which calls for counseling.

5. My fifteen-year-old daughter will do anything to be accepted. She has a hard time being accepted by different groups and changes friends often. Right now she is involved with a Hare Krishna group and is only there because she wants acceptance. I am concerned about what is going on with her, and that she will take on the values of this fanatical religious group.

This happens with many cults. They supply something which is missing in many young people's lives—security and self-esteem.

The fundamental problem your daughter has is poor self-esteem. She must have an unusually severe case of poor self-esteem and is willing to sell her values to gain this group's acceptance. Her long history of going from group to group tells us this.

Because your daughter has such a severe case of poor self-esteem, I suggest getting counseling for her. Once her self-esteem builds, she can make decisions based on her own feeling of what is right and wrong, not on a need to gain acceptance.

6. How do you get an adolescent out of a bad peer group?

It is a difficult thing to do. Again, depending on how severe it is and if these kids are actually providing dangerous situations and activities, or if you are just not happy with the overall influence, you need to do it quickly or slowly. If you do it quickly, you just tell your teenager, "I am not going to let you associate with these kids because they are into drugs and alcohol, which is unacceptable in this family."

If you want to do it more slowly and the group is not so dangerous, you need to encourage your teenager to have other friends and join other groups or activities.

7. If you have insisted that your son or daughter not associate with certain kids, how do you enforce it, for example, in school and after school until you are home from work?

It is impossible to enforce it in school because you are not there. After school though, if you feel strongly about it, you have to set up a system where the teenager cannot cheat on you. For example, make arrangements for the teen to go over to a mother's house you trust and stay there without the friend, doing homework, relaxing and watching TV until you get home from work.

8. How can we as parents confront the negative peer pressure our teenagers encounter?

Don't buy the argument that if everyone else is doing it, they should be allowed to do it as well. It may be true, but you need to tell your teenager, "These are the standards in our house which we will enforce and by which you will live."

9. My son is not very strong willed. He has a difficult time saying no. Sometimes when his friends call and it is apparent by the conversation he really does not want to do it, I tell him to say "no," and blame it on his mother. Is that OK?

Yes, as a temporary measure it is fine. For example, if his friends want him to go cruising on a Saturday night and he knows they are going to drive dangerously, you could suggest he say, "No, my mom will not let me do that. My mom will only let me go out to a specific place so she knows where I'm at." Hopefully, after a period of time, he will be able to tell his friends he does not want to do something and it will come from him, but in the meantime, using you as an excuse is fine.

10. We just moved into a new neighborhood and our twelve-year-old daughter cannot seem to make any friends. There are all sorts of little cliques and she cannot break into them.

I suggest that you have her invite a whole little clique over, even if it is from three to five girls. Have them spend the night and watch movies on the VCR. Sometimes it really works wonders to invite the whole clique over. That way, none of the others feel threatened by losing one of their friends. Invite them over for a pajama party, have pizza, watch some movies and give it a try.

CHAPTER FIVE

Allowances

It is important for the teenager that they know they have a responsibility to participate as a family member in family chores.

At this time in an adolescent's life when his behavior becomes the most troublesome because of his need to rebel, any added control is welcomed by parents. The utilization of an allowance offers this and more. It can be used to improve behavior, to teach the value of money and how to make decisions and increase responsibility. The earlier you start your child off with an allowance, the better off you are, since these values will sink in more easily at a younger age.

> *In implementing an allowance, there are right ways to do it and wrong ways. First of all, however, the amount of allowance for one or more children must fit your family's budget. Give what you can afford, but do not give in to a teen's cry that, "All my friends are getting more for allowance than me."*

In order to make your life easier and avoid the inevitable arguing and disagreements your adolescents will bring up, list the chores and goals you expect in order for them to get their allowance. Write down not only the rules of the house, but a detailed account of what is expected, so that you can stear clear of misunderstandings from the beginning. For example, you might list that Sally and John must set and clear the table for dinner on alternate days, spelling out that it includes putting all extra food in the refrigerator, rinsing off all dishes and pots, and putting them in the dishwasher, not just stacking them in the sink. Put the list on the refrigerator for all to see, so that your children cannot say they did not know what they were supposed to do. It is also important to remember not to make the list too long, tedious, or hard to understand.

Hand out allowances each week according to how many chores were done, and deducting an amount you decide for those not completed. In the event your teenagers rebel by refusing to do chores and freely forfeiting the money, tell them they have no choice. Whether or not they want the money, they must complete their chores or they will be punished.

When withholding allowance for a punishment, do not take away money not already earned. It is all right to deduct money for chores not done, but punishing your teens for bringing home bad grades or for coming home after curfew by taking away the allowance for a couple of weeks will only be counterproductive. Their motivation to do the chores will be gone. It is better to give them more chores as a punishment without taking away their ability to earn some money. If, for example, John hasn't been doing his homework on time and his grades are dropping, tell him he must show marked improvement and will be put on a progress report (see the chapter on school problems), until his grades get back up. Meanwhile, he will be punished by having to start cleaning out the garage a few hours each Saturday for a few weeks.

Adolescents have the right to certain things. They have the right to have a roof over their heads, food, and some clothes. We do not think they have the right to designer clothes, cars, or car insurance among other things. It is very important to teach teenagers the correlation between work and money.

What we suggest is that allowances be dependent on chores. Teenagers should know what chores are required of them, and, if they are completed on time, satisfactorily, then they will get their allowance. Again the allowance depends on how much you can afford, on what your income is, and on how many chores the teen does.

Questions:

1. Should you give teens additional money for birthday presents, for special activities with friends, and so forth?

That is up to you, and again, it depends on how much money you have, how well your teen is doing in school, and how well she or he obeys the rules. I certainly do not think a teen should get everything. It is appropriate to give your teenagers extra money on an "as needed" basis.

2. Would you keep up an allowance if they are working part time?

I would, if you feel you can afford it, because otherwise, you are simply punishing them for working. What you might want to consider doing is putting allowance in a savings account for special things, such as going to college, buying a car, or car insurance. I do not think it is particularly good for teens to have a lot of money in their pockets at any one time. This can lead to impulse spending, the idea that friendship can be bought, the temptation for drugs, or make them targets of being robbed.

3. What is an appropriate gift for a teenager for a birthday or for Christmas? They all want such expensive things these days.

I think the answer must depend on how much you feel you can afford. You might say to them, "Hey, here is our budget for Christmas or for your birthday (whether it is $5.00, $12.00, $25.00 or $50.00). Give us some ideas what you might like." Almost always they complain and say that is not enough. Then you might say, "Look, I am sorry you feel that way, but this is what we can afford and that is our budget."

4. Teenagers often say, "Well, you make so much money how come you cannot afford anything more?"

Teenagers usually think whatever their parents make is a lot since they have no comprehension about expenses such as mortgage, rent, food, or utilities, etc. What I suggest is that when they are around eleven or twelve years old, parents try to explain their budgets and finances in a simple way to their adolescents by sitting down with them on a regular basis. One might say, "This is how much we make, this is how much we take home after taxes, and these are what our expenses are." If teens do not understand how much you make and what taxes and expenses are, they do not really understand how much money is left for other things.

5. Why should all teens do chores?

I believe all teens should do chores because it teaches them responsibility and that every member of the family has to do things to help out the family.

6. What do you do if your teenager does not do chores?

You set a punishment and you enforce the punishment. That is part of the teen's responsibility in the family – to do chores.

7. My teenager, who is seventeen, is doing very well. He gets good grades, is in sports and activities, works outside the house in a part time job, but says he does not have time for chores.

I believe the list of chores needs to be increased or decreased, depending on the age and circumstances. I think that if a seventeen-year-old is doing well in school, involved in many activities and extra curricular sports and working, you might want to consider cutting his chores down. But I still think he should have some. It is important to let him know he is still part of the family, and everyone else does chores. So, as a family member, he still has responsibilities.

8. What if your teen does some of her chores, but not all of them?

You take away part of the money for the allowance as a punishment and add punishments until she remembers to do them all.

9. What if your teen says that he does not want the money, therefore he does not have to do chores?

Tell him that he does not have a choice, because that is part of his family responsibility and obligation. He must do chores like everyone else in the family.

10. What if your teenager wants one month or three months' allowance in advance, and you feel that they will blow it all at once?

If you think that your son or daughter can handle one or three months' allowance in advance and is very demanding and insistent, what you might want to do is offer a compromise. Say, "Look, we will give you two weeks allowance in advance, and if you prove to us you can handle it, then we will consider giving you more." Obviously if your teenager runs out of money, do not rescue her or give any more money before the end of the agreement.

CHAPTER SIX

Sibling Rivalry

The fighting and bickering between siblings can be irritating and annoying to parents when it continues day in and day out. You do not have to live in a war zone. There are definitely things which no parent should permit. These include all physical threats, swearing, name calling, and putting the other siblings down in any way. Some yelling is all right, so long as you can take it and it isn't damaging. Children need to be taught to express their feelings of anger, resentment, and envy toward siblings with words, and a parent can facilitate this.

Unfortunately, most times the opposite is true. Parents actually perpetuate the competition and comparisons which lead to the rivalry. Your children's feelings, especially during adolescence, need to be vented. You do not want this to happen in unhealthful ways, so do not just pass over your child's anger or forbid him from expressing it. Instead, acknowledge it and try to describe it, using a *"your feeling"* message (see *How To Live With Your Teenager: A Survivor's Handbook For Parents*, Chapter 4).

Comparing your children to each other can be particularly disastrous. Saying that Johnny is not as clean as his brother leads nowhere except to resentment that you don't love Johnny as much as his brother. As a result, you also hurt Johnny's self-esteem which can eventually lead to other problems. Even a positive comparison does not help anyone in the long run.

For instance, if you tell Sally she always does so much better in school than her sister, Sally will begin believing her sister is less intelligent, whether it is true or not. It is better to say exactly what you see: "Johnny, I'm afraid you need to clean up your room," and, "Sally, your grades this quarter are exceptionally good."

Another problem which can happen in a family is typecasting. The longer you or your children portray another member of the family one way, the more he or she will believe it. Is one of your children the "bully" in the family? Or is someone a "weakling" and always the butt of the other kids' jokes and pranks? As the parent, you need to open up your childrens' views of each other and their potentials. The "bully" has the capacity to be kind and the "weakling" can defend himself or herself.

It is important to help your children express their anger positively. Help them express their anger in other ways, such as by taking it out on an object like a pillow, writing their grievances down on paper, or drawing how they feel. You can get your kids to do these things by being an example to them and trying these yourself. When siblings learn how to deal with their anger, resentment, or envy toward each other, they also have a valuable and important tool which is useful the rest of their lives.

One of the most frequent questions we get at our Center is how do you stop sibling rivalry?

We need to understand what sibling rivalry is. Half jokingly, it is one of the prices you pay for having more than one child. It is natural and normal in families. There will always be rivalries and jealousy between children and teenagers for parents' love, attention, material possessions, privileges, the siblings' perception of how they are treated, and so forth.

Let's start by stating what is not acceptable:

1. Any type of physical violence towards another sibling. This includes hitting, kicking, tripping, biting, pushing, throwing things, etc.

2. Any sibling swearing at another sibling.

3. Any name calling from one sibling to another, such as stupid, dumb, idiot, faggot, jerk, four eyes and so forth.

What do you do about the "normal" everyday bickering, non-yielding and non-ending fighting (without physical violence, name-calling or swearing)? All of this often quickly gets on parents' nerves, what can you do?

You can tell your children that you are no longer willing to tolerate their bickering, and that they each need to go to their rooms for a period of time. This can be five, ten, fifteen minutes, or whatever works in your family. Afterwards, they can come out, and if they can act decently together they can stay together, otherwise, they will continue to go back to their rooms. The amount of time you as a parent can tolerate the negative interaction between siblings may depend on how your day went. If you have had a bad day at work you may not want to put up with very much; if you feel that you can tolerate it for a while, that is fine also.

Questions:

1. At what age do you begin to see the end of sibling rivalry?

If you are lucky, in the early twenties; if not, somewhere around twenty-five or twenty-six.

2. What do you do if you have explained the new rule, that there is no swearing, name-calling, putting each other down or hitting, and one of the family members breaks it?

You enforce the consequences by saying, "Hey, you know the new rule in our house. Calling your brother a name is not acceptable. I told you there were consequences." Then you follow through. Consequences can be simply taking away privileges, such as watching TV, listening to the radio or stereo, or using the computer or phone for an evening. These are sufficient consequences for the first infraction.

3. What do you do if your teenager breaks the rule again?

You escalate the consequences.

You take away the same privilege for two evenings instead of one. Remember the heart and soul of our philosophy is that parents need to be strict, they need to be firm, they need to set limits, and they need to enforce limits. You need to continue to escalate the consequences and do whatever you have to do to be in control. You as a parent set the rules of the house.

4. How do you handle a situation where one child who is four years older than the other, is very violent to the younger one, and you have told him this is not acceptable?

You tell the older one, "Your behavior is not acceptable, and as of here and now, it is going to stop. Anything I have to do to get you to stop I will do. I am not going to let you hit your brother." You set a consequence, you stick to it and you increase the consequence until the older one stops hitting the younger one. In addition, you might say "Look, I appreciate how angry you are toward your brother. Why don't you come to me and talk about it, and I will listen to you and give you another way to handle your problem through talking rather than hitting."

5. What do you do if your twelve-year-old and your three-year-old fight constantly. The twelve-year-old has many pressures that overwhelm him, and he does not get along with the three-year-old at all?

The first thing you do is set your limits and tell your twelve-year-old what he can and cannot do to the three-year-old, and tell him what will happen to him. Then you tell your twelve-year-old, "When you are unhappy, come to us. Tell us about it and we will talk, because talking about such things can help you become better. We will help you with thoughts, and we will help you with suggestions and ideas in order to overcome the problems. But taking your frustrations out on your younger brother is not acceptable, and we will not allow it."

6. I am a single mother with three children and my oldest always monopolizes all the conversation at dinner. What can I do?

The research is clear that in a three-child family, the oldest statistically will dominate 70% to 80% of the conversation at dinner. They are simply older, more mature and want all of your attention since they feel threatened by the other two.

What you can do is after he has had a chance to talk, tell him, "That is great. Now I want to speak with Sally and Bob about their day." If he interrupts, say, "Oh no, you had your turn and I will listen to more later, but now I want to hear from Sally and Bob." Then insist that the other two have their say. After you have listened to him, make sure you draw your line firmly.

7. What do you do when the oldest of three children tries to run the house?

Tell the oldest it is not his job to run the house, but your job, and you will not allow him to boss the others around.

CHAPTER SEVEN

Teenage Music

Where there are teenagers, there is music, and this music often becomes a problem for parents.

Questions:

1. Is listening to today's terrible rock music harmful to kids, and how do I get them to stop?

Much of the rock music (particularly heavy metal and punk), in my opinion, is sick and perverse. Some of it glorifies Satan and devil worship; some glorifies death and suicide; some glorifies and promotes drug usage; some glorifies sexual perversion; and some of it glorifies physical assault and murder.

The continued repeating and easy availability of such messages does nothing good, and is extremely dangerous to adolescents.

I would encourage you not to allow youngsters to listen to, or to have, the worst of the rock music in your home.

This is extremely hard to enforce because it's virtually impossible to monitor what adolescents listen to when they're alone in their room and the door is closed, when they're using earphones, when they're listening to their Walkman on the way to school, when they're in their car or friends' cars, when they're at friends' homes, etc.

The non-harmful rock music may be very loud, but it's a safe way to rebel.

2. What if I take the radio and stereo out of his room because I can't stand this music at all?

Your son will probably be extremely angry at you for it and you are only going to be able to stop him listening to it in your house. What about when he goes to a friends house, is in a friend's car, or carries his walkman with him to school? You really cannot enforce this limit, and I think enforcing it in your house is counterproductive.

3. *My sixteen-year-old son spends all his time drawing skulls and is preoccupied with death. I think it has something to do with the rock music to which he listens. Is this abnormal?*

It does not sound very healthy, if in addition to listening to the rock music, he has a preoccupation with death and drawing skulls. You should take him to a counselor for a check up since he may be severely depressed. Also, a preoccupation with death and dying can be a pre-indication of suicide. This is a serious problem and you need to immediately get counseling.

4. *How do we know whether to take our daughter to a counselor if she is listening to this terrible rock music?*

If your daughter is listening to hard rock, heavy metal, or hard core punk, but is working up to her capacity in school, has good friends whom you approve, does her chores reasonably well, is involved with an activity or participates in sports, and talks to you, then I would not be concerned. On the other hand, if she is into punk music, dresses punk and is involved with the whole subculture using drugs, then I would be very concerned and go to a counselor immediately.

CHAPTER EIGHT

Anger

Living with teenagers sometimes feels as if the parent is living in a war zone. This makes not only teenagers, but also parents angry. Here are some ways you can deal with this anger.

Questions:

1. What do you do with a teenager who is rebelling so much that you are constantly angry with him?

There are two issues. One is a battle, and one is a war. You may fight a battle with your teen on a daily basis, but to win or lose a battle is not as important as winning the war. Winning the war describes how your teenager turns out when he is twenty-five, and whether you have a good relationship with him at that age.

Do you want a relationship where you and he never see each other? Then try to win every battle every time you are together. Or, do you want one where there is closeness? Then be more patient with him, and only punish him for things which jeopardize his health, safety or welfare, and your future relationship will be good. Your feeling angry all the time is not unusual, but do not take it out on him.

I suggest that you make a list of everything your teenager does which makes you angry. Most parents could come up with between ten and twenty items. Then I suggest you pick the top three and choose those to battle, and ignore the others. That way you are concentrating on the most important things and giving your teenager room to rebel. Family ties are the most important. Work on them, and ignore little things like a messy room, loud music, ugly clothes, etc.

2. When I am firm and set limits, I feel rejected by my teenager and it makes me very angry. Do you have any suggestions about how to deal with the rejection?

It is important to understand the parent-adolescent relationship. Your job and task as a parent is not to be your children's buddy or their friend, but to be their parent. Because of the nature and process of adolescence, being a parent involves being strict. Many times your adolescent will reject you, and if he knows it bothers you, he will do it even more. That is manipulation. It goes with the turf and there is nothing you can do. Instead, by being strict, firm, and setting limits, he will respect you, and then, as he grows out of adolescence, you and he can have a different relationship and be much closer.

3. How do you get a teenager to talk her anger out? My seventeen-year-old daughter holds all her anger inside all the time.

It is important to release anger, because often when an adolescent turns her anger inside, she becomes depressed.

One thing you could do is to encourage her to write things down and keep a journal, a diary, or write a letter to you when she is angry. She does not need to show it to you or mail it, but just the process of expressing her feelings will be good for her in getting the anger out.

Also, try to create a climate in your house where you and your daughter can talk more, and then, when she feels comfortable and safe, she will let more of her anger out.

CHAPTER NINE

Compliments

Giving and accepting compliments are often difficult for teenagers.

There are skills which need to be learned by both teenagers and parents.

Questions:

1. What do you do with a child who is unwilling to accept a compliment?

Go ahead and do it anyway. Make it about a specific thing. Rather than say, "I love you because you are my son," or, "You are a really neat guy," make it about something specific. For example, "You did a great job in the yard," or "I really appreciated the way you cleaned up your room this week."

Most kids who have a hard time accepting compliments also have poor self-esteem. They need compliments very badly. It is a lot easier for teens to accept compliments, when the compliments are about something specific, since this type of compliment is less threatening.

2. Can you over compliment your kid?

Sure, you can give your teenager too many compliments. The danger in too many compliments is that your teenager can become spoiled and self-centered. You should keep everything in balance, and that includes complimenting. Letting teens do whatever they want and not setting limits also causes teens to become spoiled and self-centered.

In the same way, two pieces of chocolate might be great, but a whole box would give you a stomachache.

Again, use your judgment. However, giving too many compliments is not the problem most families have. Instead, they have problems not giving enough compliments.

3. My teenager makes me angry so often with the things she does, that I do not want to compliment her. It is also hard for me to find things to compliment her on. I do not want to give her phoney compliments. What should I do?

Do not give her false compliments, but search for something specific you can say to her, such as you like the outfit she is wearing, or her dress, or you appreciate the fact she did the dishes promptly. Make your compliments very specific.

> THEME TWO:
> How To Make Sure Your Teenager
> Doesn't Get Into Trouble

CHAPTER TEN

Jobs, Activities, Sports

How to Live With Your Teenager: A Survivor's Handbook For Parents is a specific step-by-step plan that teaches parents concrete communication skills; and then, by using the unique journal-in-the-book approach, it helps parents put these communication skills into practice. The book pioneers the idea that parenting adolescents is a skill—a skill that could be learned. The book affirms the idea that you can become a better parent as you increase your skills. The skills can be learned and increased just as you increase your skills in other areas such as cooking, gardening, or playing tennis. One of the best ways of making sure your children and adolescents don't get into trouble is to learn and utilize skills for parenting children and adolescents.

> *It is rare to find a teenager who is having medium to severe difficulties who is also involved in activities such as school activities, church youth groups, sports, part-time work, or activities after school.*

One of the things that we have noticed throughout the years is that a major difference between teenagers who do really well and those who get into a lot of trouble is that the teenager who does very well is the teenager who is very busy. They are involved in constructive activities and find these rewarding; this builds their self-esteem. It is almost a truism that if you keep your teenagers busy, they won't have time to get into trouble. One hallmark of those who have gotten into serious trouble, who drop out of school, or who have drug and alcohol problems, is that they are not involved in any activities.

One of the things you can do as a parent to ensure, as far as it is possible, that your teens do not get into trouble, is to keep them busy with activities. The earlier you start the better off they are.

Any constructive interest, hobby or activity your teenager has is good. These include church or synagogue groups, sports, school activities and clubs, clubs and classes at the recreation department, clubs and activities outside of school, such as Boy Scouts or Girl Scouts. One should also promote interests such as art, singing, dancing and computers. You can help by encouraging, talking about, and taking an active role in anything constructive in which your kid has an interest.

Questions:

1. What do you do about an eleven-year-old whose hobby of horseback riding has become an obsession?

Like everything else, things can be taken to an extreme. For example, three or four pieces of chocolate are pretty good, but a whole box would make you feel sick. What you need to do is encourage your teen to do what she loves (such as horseback riding), and then set a limit. You might say, "We are delighted that you are involved in a constructive activity and we are proud of you. It is important that you have a balance in your life. So we are going to limit the amount of time you spend with the horse, to give time for school, parents, and friends, which are also important."

2. In your experience, how important is religious faith?

My expertise is in psychology, not religion or theology, so I will answer your question from my perspective. I am 100% in favor of teenagers being involved in church or synagogue religious activities, and especially their youth groups.

3. Do you think teenagers should have a part-time job?

My belief is that the primary job of the adolescent is to go to school and work up to their capacity in school. If your teenager is doing this and wants a part-time job, I would be entirely for it. What I think the part-time job does is to teach your teenager responsibility, discipline, time management, and getting along with supervisors. The other thing it does is to promote strong self-esteem, because the teen will feel good about working, doing a job well, and earning money. If your teen is working up to capacity in school and wants a part-time job, encourage it. If your teen is not working up to capacity in school and wants a part-time job, I would negotiate some type of agreement as to what grades are needed in order to get a job or continue working, again pointing out that the primary responsibility is to work up to capacity in school.

There are some teens who are not involved in many activities, do not work up to their capacity in school, yet get an enormous amount of self-esteem from a part-time job. In these cases it is important to allow the kid to work and get their self-esteem from the job. There are certain teens who do not do well in school because of a long history of doing poorly or because of learning disabilities. It is important to allow such a child to work in order to build and promote self-esteem.

4. How do you handle an obsession with surfing that comes before sleep, work, school, or anything else?

First of all, while it may not be your favorite activity, it is constructive and helps teenagers build self-esteem. But you should set limits, since their physical health comes first and they have to get enough sleep. Secondly, they need to work up to their ability in school, and, if they are working, they need to meet their work responsibilities. You need to set limits while you support their involvement in surfing. It is important that you help them establish priorities.

5. What do I do if my teen loves snakes and wants to collect them?

This is how I handled a situation like this some time ago. I suggested to the mother that they work out a compromise where the snakes stay in cages in the garage. The adolescent involved wanted to be a veterinarian. His father became involved and once a month they went to a reptile society so the dad and son had a common interest. This became a constructive interest and that is great. Again, remember that the teen, as part of rebellion, will choose things which you do not like.

6. What do you do if your adolescent is twelve, sits around and watches eight to nine hours of TV a day, and does not have any activities, hobbies, or interests? Do you cut off TV entirely?

I am not against TV in moderation. For example, I think teens after school are entitled to watch TV or do something of their choice to relax. I do think eight to nine hours of TV is not at all productive. What I would suggest is limit the TV to one hour a day and say, "Look, part of my responsibility as your parent is to help you develop activities and interests. I am going to insist you choose one activity and do it. You can have your choice. We will get a list of activities at the local YMCA or YWCA and other clubs and see what they offer, and also look at those which are available at your school. You can be in a club after school or during school, you can choose any activity that might interest you, but I am going to insist you choose one. We do not care if it is karate lessons or tennis lessons, a church youth group, or anything constructive."

7. What do you do if your adolescent is seventeen and you use the same approach and it does not work?

If your teen has never been involved in activities and spends most of the time watching TV, you can still try this. But I would not force it on a seventeen-year-old because you may not have the power to do it. However, you can certainly enforce limiting TV.

8. What do you do about a seventeen-year-old who does not have any activities or interests and sits around all summer driving her mother crazy and does not want to get a job?

I certainly would encourage her to get a job. I think you might want to consider finding out why she is not able to get a job. You might check with her and see if it is because she is afraid to get an interview. She may not know how to get an interview, she may not know how to fill out an application, or she may not know how to ask for an application. If any of these are an issue or problem, work with her on each one. The other thing you could do with a seventeen-year-old who hangs around the house and refuses to work is certainly not give her money; and if she wants money, insist that she has to earn it herself.

9. How do you deal with younger teenagers, asking them to get involved with church youth groups and sports, when they see real people involved in sex scandals and money scandals on TV? They see many professional athletes today using drugs and sometimes dying from overdoses.

While certainly the papers are full of problems reported in some ministries, as well as with athletes having drug problems, I think overall, churches and synagogues provide excellent and outstanding leaders for youth groups. You need to educate your teenagers to the problems of drugs and the fact that sometimes the role models and sports heroes have drug problems as well. It could help you reinforce how dangerous drugs are.

10. How much pressure can a boy take with school sports, activities, and jobs? Can teens become too busy?

Of course, there are always problems with anything in extreme. Some teens take on so much that they feel enormous pressure and stress, and this can lead to depression. It is your responsibility as a parent to keep in touch with what is going on in your teen's life and monitor his behavior. If you sense there is too much pressure and stress, you can help. If your teen shows any signs or symptoms of pressure and stress, you would need to sit down with him and insist he drop some activities and emphasize that school work should always be the first priority.

11. What can I do to get my teenagers busy in the summer?

If they are of working age you might encourage part time jobs. If the school offers summer school you might encourage that. You can check with your local colleges and universities to see if they offer courses for teenagers. Also, check with your city recreation department. But again I think it is very bad to have teens inactive during the summer—they should be doing something specific.

CHAPTER ELEVEN

Contracts

Almost all adolescents feel helpless. One reason they feel helpless is because they are told what to do by parents, teachers, coaches, and bosses. One way to get them to cooperate much better is with a contract. A contract works by you and your adolescent coming to an agreement and signing a written statement. You can start by sitting down together and listening to what each of you wants, and then negotiating.

(The exact formulation for this and details concerning contracts are covered in Chapter 9 in my book, *How To Live With Your Teenager: A Survivor's Handbook For Parents*.)

> In a contract, teenagers are involved in the decision-making process which affects them. You can negotiate chores or just about any type of conflict which does not affect health, safety, and welfare. Again, if teens have a say in what they are doing, they usually respond better. When you make the contract, however, it needs to be made clear that the parents are the final boss. If there is a dispute, the parents' word goes.

Questions:

1. What are some of the issues which come up in family contracts?

Typical issues teenagers bring up are a change of bedtime, curfew, or chores. Typical issues for parents are wanting chores done, rooms picked up, curfews met, and better school grades.

2. Could you explain a little bit more how the contract works?

Sure, the first step is explaining what each person wants. For example, let us say the teenager goes first and states that he or she would like to go to bed at 10:30 P.M. instead of 9:30. The parent repeats the request to make sure he or she has heard it accurately, and then makes one of three choices. One is to say yes, one is to say no, and the other is to offer a compromise. Say you compromise with 10:00. It is written down and signed. I find when people sign a contract and are told it is now a "law," they are more likely to live up to it.

3. What do you do with a seventeen-year-old who signed a written agreement not to drink with the sports team he's involved with at school, but goes ahead and drinks? He says 90% of the kids drink and use drugs. How do you handle that?

Number one, tell him that just because everyone does it does not make it right, even if it is, in fact, true 90% of the kids use drugs and drink. If everyone jumped into the ocean in the middle of winter, it does not mean he should also. Tell him it is not acceptable to use alcohol, and you will not allow it.

4. My daughter wants to use a little bit of marijuana and wants to negotiate a contract with that. What do I do?

Anything which concerns health, safety, or welfare is a nonnegotiable contract and not up for discussion. Smoking marijuana is an issue of health as well as legality, so just say simply that it is not negotiable, and you are not going to allow her to smoke marijuana. If you have a swimming pool and she wanted to negotiate running on the pool deck, that is not negotiable either, because it is a matter of safety. Things which are negotiable are curfew, chores, allowances, where your teenager can go, when she can go there, how she can go, and clothes, etc.

5. What can be done about a ten-year-old who is doing well in sports and school but rebelling at home?

You might try making some contracts at home for his behavior. For example, if you find he hates to take the trash out, you might try to get another family member who wants to take the trash out, and switch chores. Again, if you have some agreement from him and he participates in the decisions which affect his life, he will usually be much more cooperative and less likely to rebel.

6. What do you do with a girl who makes an agreement to practice an hour a day with her piano lessons which we pay for, and she breaks the agreement?

You give her a week's warning and say, "If you do not practice, then we will discontinue the lessons," and then do so if she doesn't practice.

CHAPTER TWELVE

Discipline and Punishment

The heart and soul of our philosophy is that parents need to be strict, they need to be firm, they need to set limits, and hold to their limits. We have found that parents who set strict guidelines for their kids have the healthiest teenagers. One of the questions which comes up most often is how do I punish my adolescent? We'll address this issue in this chapter.

> *The biggest difference between kids who seem to do real well and kids who have a lot of problems is that the kids who do real well come from families where parents are very strict. We believe firmly in strictness, discipline, and punishment. Parents must be in control of their teenagers at all times.*

Because it is so difficult to raise a teenager today, between 30% to 40% of the parents we see in our office have a teenager who is in some way out of control. For example, they won't go to school, come in and go out as they please, or do not obey any rules in the home. Later, we will talk about how to get your teenager back into control.

For a punishment, you want to start with taking a privilege away for an evening which would be something important to the teenager, such as the computer, the Nintendo, phone, stereo, radio, or TV. If the punishment does not work, you take the privilege away for two evenings, and escalate on up until the teenager gets back into control and the negative behavior stops.

For most parents, there is a pattern in the house of the teenagers getting away with more than they should. It is important to break the pattern and get back into control for your child's best interest. In setting a new pattern, there will be some turmoil, but you need to stick to your guns and punish until you get the result you want.

Questions:

1. My daughter's room is incredibly messy, with clothes all over the floor, etc. This is the one thing I hate the most and it is giving me a stomachache. She has one activity which she really enjoys, horseback riding. Should I not allow her to go in order to punish her for her messy room? If I take anything else away, she would not care.

In Chapter 2 of *How To Live With Your Teenager, A Survivors Handbook For Parents*, I described age-appropriate behaviors of adolescents, including safe and unsafe ways to rebel. My own feeling is that having a messy room is really a safe way to rebel, although you think it important that she pick it up. However, it is more important to understand that this is a safe form of rebellion. What happens too often is that parents clamp down so hard on the safe ways to rebel that they literally force their kids into unsafe ways to rebel. If you take her TV away and she does not care, then you might consider a punishment designed to make your daughter do some extra work or go to bed earlier. But in regards to her horseback riding, I would be very reluctant in taking it away, since activities such as this are beneficial to an adolescent's self-esteem. There are many things I would not take away, such as church or synagogue youth group activities and school activities such as band and sports. Do not take away activities that help adolescents feel good about themselves and build self-esteem.

2. My eleven-year-old has an attitude problem. Every time I tell her something she dislikes, she acts as if she were having a seizure. Her eyes roll back, her head goes back and she appears as if I am torturing her.

Well, to me that is safe rebellion. For example, wouldn't you rather have that than drugs, alcohol, or running away? Let's go over the definition of safe rebellion. The definition of safe rebellion is behavior which usually results in making you angry and having your stomach in a knot. In order to make a successful transition from childhood to adulthood, the adolescent must rebel against adult norms and morals. So if your stomach is in a knot most of the time, your teenager is doing his job right. In your case, your child's apparent seizures seem to be getting the desired results of teen rebellion. But do not despair, since she will certainly grow out of it.

3. My twelve-year-old is like the daughter of the woman who asked the previous question. What I do is to slap her really hard a couple of times, which usually makes the situation better.

I am thoroughly against hitting children once they are older than seven or eight. Hitting your adolescent will eventually backfire, particularly when you hit a kid older than nine. While you may get the immediate result you want, it creates a deep, inner anger and humiliation. During adolescence, kids begin thinking of themselves as adults, and to use discipline of a physical nature like slapping or hitting, which you would never use against another adult, is devastating to the adolescent's self-esteem. I have never seen hitting or slapping a child over ten as anything other than counterproductive. While it may be an immediate solution, it creates more problems in the long run than you could have ever imagined.

So if all your child does during adolescence is to role her eyes, fake seizures and look at you as if she wanted to kill you, then you are very fortunate.

4. How do I enforce consequences, such as taking the TV away, when I am a working mother, and neither my husband or I get home until 6:30 p.m.?

Do not make threats you cannot enforce. For example, if you are going to take the TV away, there is really no way of enforcing it if the teen comes home from school and knows you won't get home until 6:30. Instead, select consequences that go into effect after dinner when you can enforce them. You could take the TV away, or lock it up somehow while you are at work, which is OK too, but it is up to you to decide, depending on how much inconvenience you are willing to put up with.

5. How can I ground my teenager after school and enforce it if I get home from work at 6:00 p.m.?

Insist he must be home after school, and to be sure, you are going to call randomly until you get home. If there is a phone call, he is not to stay on the phone for more than ten seconds. Call a couple of times, and if he does not answer, he will be punished again.

6. What do you think of leaving the choice of punishment up to the teenager?

It is not a good idea since she may choose something too easy or even too hard. If you have a parenting style where you involve the teenager, asking her which punishment she wants from a list, it is important to let her know that while her input is welcome, you are going to make the final decision.

7. What if punishments such as taking away the TV, phone, computer, stereo, or radio do not seem to bother my teenagers?

They may be bluffing and really do care, but are not going to let you know. Another solution would be to give them extra chores which most kids dislike.

8. What if my teenager wants to know the reason for everything he is told to do?

You do not have to put up with such behavior, so when you have had enough you can tell your teenager, "Your behavior is inappropriate and I feel you are trying to manipulate me. So stop the questioning." Or you might limit him to three questions a day.

9. What if you follow through with consequences and your teen gives you the cold shoulder?

You ignore it. The adolescent may be trying to make you feel guilty, or she may just be sulking or need some time alone.

10. How do you reconcile being strict with an adolescent's need to rebel?

You try to keep your teen's rebellion to areas that are safe. While it is important for chores to be done and rooms to be clean, you can allow for some standard less than perfection. Again, if your adolescent's only faults are not doing chores, or having a messy room, you are extremely lucky.

You need to allow for some rebellion and some imperfection, but you can also request chores to be done and rooms picked up. On the other hand, if you clamp down too hard you can literally force your kid into an unsafe rebellion.

11. What can you do about a teenager who belches or slurps in public, and how do you punish that?

I suggest you give an "I" message to the effect, "I feel uncomfortable when someone I am with and who I care about belches or slurps in public." Another option is, if your goal is to take your kid out and have a good time, I would wait until you get home to say that, and not embarrass him in public. At home you might say, "Hey, I want to give you some feedback," and give the kid the "I" message at home.

12. My parents are coming in for a week and my fifteen-year-old daughter states that she is not going to talk to them because they are old fashioned, strict, and don't understand teenagers. I am worried about a possible conflict, because my parents are very critical and do not understand teenagers at all. Almost every word they utter is critical about my daughter, her music, and lifestyle.

Tell her you understand how difficult your parents are, but that they are set in their ways and are not going to change. You are aware of how uncomfortable their criticism makes her and how unfair they are. In the same token, she is to be polite to them and spend a little time each day talking to them, which is her responsibility as a family member. End by saying that she will be punished if she does anything other than that.

13. I agree with what you are saying, but I have never done much follow through. How do I start?

Give your teenager a warning by saying, "There are going to be new rules in our house, and if you break these rules you are going to have these immediate consequences." He will not believe you since you have never done it before, so the next time a rule is broken you must follow through and punish him.

14. My wife and I never agree on punishments. When I give them, my wife will not enforce them, or sometimes she will change the punishments after I give them.

Often wives and husbands do not agree on punishments since we are all individuals and have many different opinions. What is crucial is that parents present a single front to teenagers. This is very important. Otherwise, a teenager might manipulate one parent against the other, which is not good for the teenager. What you need to do is to go behind closed doors and work out a compromise with which you both can live, and then enforce it and back each other up.

15. My sixteen-year-old daughter went to a party and was supposed to be back by 10:30, but came home at midnight. To me this is very serious, so why shouldn't I ground her for two months?

What we recommend is start by grounding her for a shorter period of time, and if she breaks the rule again, make it longer. In the life of a teenager, two months is an awfully long time, and that type of rule-breaking doesn't deserve such a long punishment for the first time.

16. Should kids have chores?

Absolutely. It teaches them responsibility, and that every member of the family has to participate in helping the family. They should have chores from a very young age.

17. How do you get kids to do chores?

Often with great difficulty. One of the most effective ways is to make a "Notice of Chores" to be put on the refrigerator, listing them by child and day. For example, Monday, Wednesday, Friday, and Sunday, John clears the table. Tuesday, Thursday, Saturday, Sally clears the table. Also, list times by which things need to be done. Thus, every Tuesday, John takes trash out by 9:00 p.m. Dishes are to be put away from the dishwasher by 8:00 p.m.

18. What if they do not do their chores by the designated time?

You follow through with your selected consequences, such as taking away part of their allowance.

19. You talk a lot about punishment and restrictions. What about rewards?

I am a great believer in rewarding kids. You can reward kids by giving them praise. Most everyone likes receiving praise and compliments. You can praise kids for the way they look, achievements in school, being nice to you, doing chores, getting a good mark on a paper, or doing well in an event or activity.

Praise is the easiest way to reward kids. Another way is by spending time with them or doing special things together. For example, you could buy a special gift, which need not be expensive, to show your appreciation of your adolescent's achievements.

20. My teenager does not complete his chores. He always puts them off "another minute" until the day is over and they are not done. What can I do?

If you make a list of the chores and put it on the refrigerator you would not have that problem, since your teen would know specifically when chores had to be done. If he does not follow this, you punish. The only exceptions to the deadlines are those you allow.

21. I am continually exhausted by my teenager's need to be

reminded of her chores.

One of the age-appropriate behaviors of adolescents which I have discussed is testing. To avoid this, follow the advice of the previous question by making a list of chores.

22. Is not doing chores safe rebellion?

Yes. Just realize that while it is irritating, frustrating, and exhausting to get your teen to do chores, wouldn't you rather have your kid refuse to do them than to use drugs, alcohol, or run away?

23. What can I do when my fifteen-year-old daughter says she is going to run away because I disciplined her?

Tell her, "That way of talking to me is not acceptable. If you are angry, tell me, and we will sit down and talk about it. I will not tolerate being threatened by you, but I will listen to your feelings. If you feel you are so unhappy you need to run away, sit down and tell me and we will talk about it, but I am not going to accept that as a threat."

24. My teenager is always lying. Should I punish him for this?

Almost all teenagers lie, basically because they are afraid to tell the truth. There are a number of things you can do for this. One is to establish a climate where the teen feels comfortable telling the truth.

Since adolescents perceive their parents as being judgmental and critical, they are often afraid to say things they know will displease their parents.

Another way to handle this is to tell your teen that you want an answer to a question, and she has the option either of not telling you anything or telling you the truth, and that you will not punish her for not saying anything. Or, you could say, "Tell me the truth. I won't punish you whatever it is." If you go this route, you must be willing to tolerate information which will displease you. For example, if you ask your teenage daughter to tell you if she is having sex. If you promise not to punish her, then be ready to help her if she says yes. Of course, if you go back and punish, then you have broken all trust and she will not tell you the truth anymore.

25. Do you take away more than one privilege at one time, and how long do I enforce a punishment?

It depends upon the infraction. I would suggest starting with one and working your way up. Concerning how long, I would start with a day and raise it if the teenager continues to misbehave.

26. What do I do when my twelve-year-old son copies his eighteen-year-old brother's rebellious behavior by not doing his chores?

The twelve-year-old says, "My brother doesn't have to, I don't have to either."

You crack down on both of them. You tell your twelve-year-old that, yes, it is a problem that his older brother is not doing his chores and you will deal with him, but you are going to deal with him separately. They are two separate issues and he will do his chores, or get punished likewise.

With the older brother it is a different issue since you do not have to support him legally after eighteen. Our position is clear: as long as you allow the older son in your house, he has to obey your rules. He does not have to live there, but, if he does, he must obey your rules. Make it clear to the eighteen-year-old that he must obey your rules if he is to stay. Say, "If you are unhappy we will certainly discuss things with you and listen to anything you have to say. We are the parents and are going to set the rules. If we cannot agree, you could leave."

Then, if he does not do the chores, ask him to leave, but only if you are willing to call the bluff.

When I say this, most parents look at me with horror. I know that most of the mothers and fathers will not do this. They will not force their child to leave if he is not obeying the rules of the house. But, you are not really helping your teenager if you allow him to stay yet do not require him to be responsible.

27. My kid swears at me all the time. Is this safe rebellion?

No. You should not, as a parent, allow yourself to be called names or to be sworn at by your child, since it is detrimental to the child should it continue, not to mention infuriating to you. So if it happens again, punish her and follow through, since she will probably not believe you.

28. What do you do about an unmotivated high school graduate who will not go to work? He gets up, watches TV all day, and then goes out and has a few beers with his friends in the evening.

You tell him he must do something constructive, such as working, going to school, going to college, or taking some job training courses, or he will have to leave. Give him thirty days to get involved in something constructive. When the thirty days are over, put all his stuff outside and take away his key.

You are not helping by allowing him to stay home: you are doing him a disservice. It does not teach him anything, and you are contributing to his problems.

The other option is to recognize his unmotivated behavior as a problem which needs counseling, and then offer him professional help through that.

29. What do you do when something gets broken in the house and no one will accept responsibility for breaking it?

If something gets broken because of horsing around or throwing a ball inside, tell them you want to know about it. If they tell you, their punishment will be less, otherwise, you will have to punish them all.

30. I have two children who are four years apart, and the older one is very violent with the younger despite my warnings to stop. What can I do?

Tell your older adolescent there is probably something behind his hitting his younger brother. You really want him to talk about it, but abusing his brother will not be tolerated. Do everything you must to make him stop. One thing you might do if you are a working mother is not to allow him in the house until you get home.

31. What if he still hits his younger brother while I am at home?

You tell him that this is not going to happen again. You take the door off of his room and put it in the garage or a friend's garage. Take everything out of his room except a couple changes of clothes and a mattress and say, "Look, this is for starters. Things will only get worse if you do not stop the hitting. I am going to be in control and am not going to allow you to hit your brother. I'll do whatever it takes to stop this." If he does not respond to this, I would suggest getting him into counseling.

32. When I punish my teenage daughter by restricting a privilege or grounding her, she tries to avoid it or ignores the punishment.

If she defies your punishment, you can make the punishments longer or give another one. You could try to give punishments that cause the least amount of aggravation to you. For example, you could take away the TV, and enforce it by putting it in the garage or locking it up.

33. I made an agreement with my sixteen-year-old son that if he borrowed my tools, he would put them away by 5:00 p.m. He knows how much my tools mean to me, and yet, he cannot even respect this. The night he left them out, I punished him by grounding him for the evening. That night he happened to have a special date with his girlfriend and her family for a party, so he became furious. We almost got into a fight. He ran out of his room and stayed away for four hours. Things have not been right since then. Didn't I have the right to punish him?

Yes, you did, but there are other ways to approach the situation. Parenting styles are different as people are different. An alternative might have been to punish him on a different night since the party was very important to him. If he is still holding a grudge because of your decision, say, "Look, I am really hurt when someone I love is holding a grudge against me. Let's talk about it."

34. How do you punish a teenager when she stays out all night?

First of all, try to find out what happened. Did she go to a party or get drunk? Is there any indication that there is a greater problem? Once you find out the story, it seems that being grounded for two weeks might be an appropriate punishment for staying out all night.

35. Our daughter is busy with cheerleading, band and church youth groups, and doesn't seem to have a second to spare. Should we make her do chores?

I think it is important for kids to do chores because it shows that the family must work together and that everyone needs to contribute. It also teaches kids responsibility. It is great that she is so busy. As I said before, busy kids rarely get into trouble. So, I would ask her to do chores at free times, such as the weekend. Chores like vacuuming, dusting, cleaning her bathroom and her room would not be overburdensome.

36. In grounding, what kind of limitations should we impose?

It depends on how strict you want to be. One type of grounding is not letting the child go out of the house, yet allowing the use of the TV, phone, stereo, computer, and so forth. Another type of grounding is denying the use of privileges at home. For most kids, grounding is a pretty serious punishment, so in most circumstances, it would be OK to let them use the stereo, etc.

CHAPTER THIRTEEN

Limits and Setting Limits

Again, our philosophy is that parents need to be strict, they need to be firm, they need to set limits and enforce limits. From my experience, it is clear that parents who are strict and firm have children who are better adjusted than parents who aren't.

Questions:

1. How do you handle an obsession with surfing that comes before sleep, work, school or anything else?

Well, I have good news and bad news. Any adolescent who has an activity which keeps him busy, is constructive and healthy, will rarely get into trouble with school, drugs, alcohol, or the criminal justice system. I do not care if it is an athletic team, band, karate, art lessons, church or synagogue youth group or anything else the teenager likes which is positive, and that includes surfing. Your job as a parent in this situation is to set limits.

The parents are the boss in the home. Your child's physical health comes first. He needs to get a certain amount of sleep each night. School comes second, where he should be working up to his ability. I would also suggest there be some balance with other things, such as some time with his parents, etc. He probably has friends if he is going surfing. If he is doing chores and working up to his capacity in school, I would see the surfing as a positive activity. If not, set limits and insist he follow them before he surfs.

2. What do you do when you have a teenager who threatens to run away and actually goes out into the street trying to make you feel guilty whenever you set a limit?

You tell her there is a rule in your house. Acting like that and threatening to run away is unacceptable. If she wants to discuss how she feels when you set rules, that is fine. Make it clear such behavior will not be tolerated. This type behavior should be punished.

3. What are proper limits to set for a daughter who is eighteen and finished high school?

The adolescent should be doing something. She should not be idle at home but involved in something constructive, which would include going to college, a trade school, or working. The adolescent should also have some chores. You have the right to set limits while she is living in your house, such as curfews, chores, or who she has over.

On the other hand, it is not proper for eighteen-year-olds to come in at 4:00 a.m. every Friday and Saturday. If they insist on doing those things, fine. Let them go live on their own. If you do not want them smoking in your house, they cannot smoke; if you want the living room picked up at the end of the day, they have to do that. It is your house, you set the rules.

4. What do you do if your teenager does not take the trash out even after being reminded several times?

You punish him by taking away a privilege, such as the phone, TV, computer, radio, or stereo for a day. If he still does not listen, then the following day you escalate the punishment and make it for two days. However, do not ground the kid for two weeks for a simple infraction such as not taking out the trash.

If you have not set or enforced limits before, he will not believe you. So, warn him in advance, since he will more than likely break the limit. Then go ahead and punish him.

5. Should I let my fifteen-year-old daughter take the bus to the beach and spend all day Saturday there? What type of limits should I set?

If you have any suspicion your kid uses drugs or alcohol, do not let her go. If you do not have these suspicions and she does reasonably well in school, gets along well at home, has nice friends whom you know and feel good about and you trust her, consider letting her go for four hours, then six, then all day. Let her know it is a privilege, and if she does anything which gives you a reason not to trust her, then do not let her go. This also depends on whether you feel your fifteen-year-old is mature enough to spend the day at the beach without getting into trouble.

6. What can I do with my nine-year-old daughter whose closest friend lies, curses, swears, and encourages my daughter to do the same?

You have the right and obligation as a parent to tell your daughter you do not want her associating with such a person and tell her why. I would say to her, "Hey, we are against such behavior, and it is our responsibility either not to allow you to be with her or to severely limit your time with her, and we will help you in finding new friends."

7. My son listens to hard rock music which talks about Satan and devil worship which I find disgusting and know is a bad influence on him. How do I get him to stop?

You can tell him your feelings and request that he stop. But it is virtually impossible, since you cannot enforce what he listens to in his room or on the way to and from school or in a friend's car or home. I do not believe in setting limits you cannot enforce. All you can do is make your position clear and hope for the best.

Research on this subject says music which is Satanic does not have a negative influence on an adolescent unless he is already into devil worship, which is another problem altogether.

8. We only have one phone and our daughter uses it after dinner at 6:30 until 9:30 when she goes to bed. What do we do?

You set a limit. Depending on how many other people are in the house, you might say something like, "Hey, because we only have one phone and your dad and I need to receive calls, each of you can use the phone only fifteen minutes per hour," or whatever is comfortable for you. After you have set your limit, stick to it and make your children stick to it.

9. We have a separate phone for our daughter; should we limit the use of it or not?

If her chores and homework are done and she is working up to her capacity in school, I would allow her unlimited use of the phone, which would be age-appropriate. If her chores are not done, I would insist they be done first. If her work is not up to where it should be in school, I would limit her phone usage severely, perhaps to half an hour or forty-five minutes per night until her work is up to what she is capable of doing.

10. Should a girl who has just graduated from high school, is attending junior college and living at home, have a curfew?

Absolutely. Anytime someone lives in your house, you have a right to demand and expect them to obey the rules. She should have a curfew as well as chores.

11. What do we do about our son who is an only child and gets many material things? He is getting more and more demanding.

Sit down with him and tell him, "Look, here is what we can afford from our budget for clothes and entertainment. We will be happy to give you a certain amount of money for an allowance each week, but that is all we can give." If he screams or complains, let him, but stick to your limits. It is helpful to let adolescents know the value of money and that there are limitations to it according to your budget.

12. If I set a lot of limits, I am afraid my daughter might be angry at me and not like me.

The most appropriate function of the parent is to be a parent, not a buddy. If kids do not like you, that is OK. What they need much more than liking a parent is to respect the parent. They will not respect you if you do not set limits and let them get away with murder.

13. Our daughter is obsessed with designer clothes, and she would rather have one item from Nordstrom's rather than ten from Sears. We give her a set amount for clothes every month, but she has very few items and we worry about it.

I think you are doing well. Give your daughter a budget for clothes and it is her decision if she wants to spend her money for one expensive item rather than ten moderately priced items.

It may be that she is in a peer group where they wear nothing but designer clothes, and she feels very uncomfortable if she does not have the clothes her friends wear. This is typical for teenagers. If that is the case, you might want to talk to her sometime about options and choices, and what values are really important in peoples' lives. You want to give her some options, but since the peer group is so important in adolesence, she may still feel compelled to wear what her peer group is wearing.

14. I am a working mother. How can I get my kids to study in the afternoon when they come home from school, when there is no one around to enforce it?

I do not believe in giving limits you cannot enforce. When kids first come home from school I do not think they should be made to study. They have been sitting in classrooms all day and may need to run around and play, watch TV, listen to the stereo, or do something else other than study. You can encourage them to study after school and tell them if they get their homework done, they won't have to do it in the evening, but you can only insist that they set aside study time when you are home.

15. How do I answer my teen's frequent complaint that, "All my friend's parents give them more money, or a later curfew?"

You simply tell them, "We are a different family and have different rules in our house. Just because your friend's parents do something doesn't mean we should."

16. What do I do when my sixteen-year-old son says he is going party hopping on Saturday evening?

You tell him that is not acceptable and you are not going to let him do it. Often at such adolescent parties, there are drugs and alcohol downstairs, and sex upstairs. If your son wants to go to a party, then I suggest you call first to make sure parents will be there. You need to know the phone number and address, and tell your son he has got to be there the whole time because you may call to check, or pop in. You need to know there will be no alcohol or drugs.

17. What do you do when you have four children and one of them wants to talk to you alone, but the others always appear and want the attention too?

Make it clear to the other three that you are talking to Sally right now and will be glad to talk to them later, but they need to leave because you are going to spend time with her alone. Then you insist it happen.

18. What can I do when every time I set limits for my son, he threatens to go live with his father?

Tell him if he wants to live with his father, you will be glad to sit down and talk about it. However, it is not acceptable for him to make threats or try to manipulate you, and if he does it again, you will have to punish him.

19. I have a problem with my teenager daughter. She is constantly taking things of mine to wear. She took a pair of earrings, lost them, and now I am making her pay for them

out of her allowance and part-time job. Am I being too strict?

No. Set your limits and keep to them. You are teaching her a valuable lesson, that you must not take things without asking first, and that you must replace something you have lost.

20. Whenever I set a limit, my son says, "I wish I were dead." I cannot stand being around him anymore. What should I do?

Whenever you hear an adolescent make any type of suicide statement (this is clearly one), it is extremely important to pay attention to it. I would go to him after you have calmed down and say, "You will not use that type of statement when you are angry, it is totally unacceptable. If you really feel that way, come and talk to me about it because I am very concerned."

21. How do you deal with a child who back talks all the time and is disrespectful?

It depends on what you consider back talk, and how much you can tolerate in your parenting style. It is certainly inappropriate to allow a child to call you any derogatory name or swear at you. For example, such disrespect as calling you stupid, dumb, idiot, or swearing at you, should never be tolerated.

I consider teenagers yelling at parents, "I hate you," or "I am really angry at you," as a relatively safe form of rebellion, and would encourage you to tolerate it if you can. If not, set your limit and say you will not allow certain things to be said against you, that they are unacceptable, and that you will have to punish them if the rule is not followed.

22. Whenever my wife and I are in the family room watching TV, our teenagers always talk to each other and make jokes which disturbs us greatly. What can we do?

Tell them they are welcome to stay and watch the program, but are not allowed to talk or joke during the program because you cannot hear or enjoy it. Set your limit and enforce it.

23. We have cable TV and there are certain movies we do not want the kids watching that have heavy sexual content and violence. They are twelve and thirteen. What do we do?

Do not allow the kids to watch movies you think are unappropriate for them.

24. How much freedom should a fourteen-year-old have in the summer? During the summer, our son goes to a friend's

home. The parents work and are not home until 6:00 o'clock at night.

It depends on the adolescent. If you trust him, if he does well in school and has friends you approve of, you could give him more freedom than if he weren't trustworthy.

You can tell him you need to know where he is going each day. He needs to give you a phone number or address of the place he is going to be, and the time he'll return.

CHAPTER FOURTEEN

Trust

Trusting teenagers is an issue most families struggle with. Here are some typical questions about freedom and trust.

Questions:

1. How much freedom should a fourteen-year-old have in the summer?

It depends on the adolescent. If you feel he is doing well in school, working up to his ability, and has good friends, then he has given you no reason not to trust him and you could give him a lot a freedom. But if you do not approve of his friends, or think there is a problem with drugs or alcohol, do not trust him, and say that until he has earned your trust, he will be under strict rules.

If he goes to a friend's house, you need to know which friend and have a phone number. Tell him you will check up on a regular basis. You can insist on meeting his friends, too. Remember, the heart and soul of our philosophy is that parents need to be strict, firm, and set and keep their limits.

An untrustworthy teenager will tell you repeatedly he is going over to one friend's house, while he is really out getting into trouble. If you trust your son, that is fine. If not, then make him call you and check in, and ask permission every time he wants to make a change. If he does not follow the rules, ground him until he obeys.

2. My teen says that I will embarrass him if I call parents and check up on him.

Tell him it is his problem, and that until he earns your trust, you are going to check on him on a regular basis. If he really has a problem with it, tell him to blame it on you and say you are a kooky and difficult parent.

3. How much trust should I give my teenager?

You either trust your teenager or you don't. If you trust your teen, you will believe them until there is a reason not to.

4. Now that my teenage son has his own car, how can I trust him short of following him around twenty-four hours a day?

Again, you either trust him or you don't. If you trust him, then give him freedom to go places so long as you know where he is. If you don't trust him, then severely limit the use of his car until he earns your trust.

CHAPTER FIFTEEN

Inpatient Treatment

There are times when outpatient visits with a therapist are not enough to bring about desired changes in a teen's severely depressed feelings, suicidal or out-of-control behavior, drug or alcohol addiction, and other problems.

> *In my own practice of therapy, I have worked with hundreds of teens who did not respond to one or more hours of counseling a week. Even if they truly wanted to change their behavior and cooperate in the therapy sessions, they were unable to make good progress because the treatment wasn't intensive enough.*

Consider that there are 168 hours in a week. If even two hours are spent in therapy and another 56 hours are spent sleeping, that still leaves 110 hours each week in which the teens must use their own resources to get along with family, meet responsibilities for household chores, get themselves off to school, pay attention, learn what's taught, do homework, engage in constructive hobbies and sports, and get along with friends.

Some teens don't have the resources, skills, or self-control to handle these 100 hours without drinking or using drugs, cutting school, committing criminal acts, engaging in violent or self-destructive acts, or creating serious disruptions in their families' lives. These teens obviously need a more structured environment where they can learn the necessary self-control, skills and resources they need to live productively. They need a top-quality inpatient program.

If a teen's out-of-control behavior or serious depression has continued over a period of many months, even years, he has developed deep habits that are unlikely to change without intensive, highly-focused treatment. That is exactly what is available in a good inpatient program designed especially for adolescents.

My own practice is based in Southern California, where I have utilized College Hospital and College Hospital Costa Mesa for my patients who need inpatient treatment. I choose College Hospital and College Hospital Costa Mesa for my adolescent patients because they offer all the components that are necessary to help teens gain the skills they need to succeed. Those components are described in several of the answers to questions asked later in this chapter.

Mental health professionals agree that it's always best to use treatment approaches that give the patient the greatest level of freedom they can handle and which causes the least disruption in the family's normal lifestyle. No responsible therapist would recommend inpatient treatment for all teens who need professional help, but for some teens inpatient treatment is the best choice if they are to have any chance at success. For some, it may be their only chance.

Questions:

1. When is inpatient treatment considered necessary?

Inpatient treatment is necessary when a teenager is suicidal and life is in jeopardy. It is often necessary when a teenager is addicted to alcohol or drugs, or is totally out of control. Although outpatient therapy is the preferred method of treatment for most teens, specific cases may need inpatient therapy. In those instances, your therapist can discuss with you what treatment method is recommended and why.

2. How can I tell for sure if my teen needs to be hospitalized?

You probably can't tell for sure. If your car makes strange noises and performs erratically, you know something's wrong with it, even though you don't know exactly what needs to be done to make it better. The logical thing is to take it to a mechanic, who is trained to inspect the car and tell you exactly what needs to be done.

When your teen makes strange noises and performs erratically, the logical thing is to consult a therapist, who is trained to diagnose the problems and recommend a specific approach to treatment. For some teens, the therapist will recommend outpatient treatment, for some he'll recommend family counseling, for some he'll recommend educational therapy, and for others he'll recommend inpatient therapy.

3. How can I tell if my teen is suicidal?

Here are some warning signs of adolescent suicide. If your teenager ever displays any warning signs of adolescent suicide, immediately rush your teenager to a therapist for an evaluation.

- Noticeable change in eating habits
- Withdrawal from friends and family and regular activities
- Persistent boredom
- A decline in the quality of schoolwork
- Violent or rebellious behavior
- Running away
- Drug and alcohol abuse
- Unusual neglect of personal appearance
- Difficulty concentrating
- Radical personality change
- Complaints about physical symptoms often related to emotions, such as stomachache, headache, fatigue, etc.
- Giving verbal "hints" with statements such as "I won't be a problem for you much longer," "Nothing matters," or "It's no use."
- Putting his/her affairs in order, for example, giving away favorite possessions, cleaning his/her room, throwing things away, etc.
- Becoming suddenly cheerful after a period of depression.

4. Why is inpatient treatment so much better than outpatient treatment?

It isn't always. If a teen's problems are only mild to moderate, and he's doing well in outpatient treatment, then he doesn't need inpatient treatment. If he is out of control, abuses alcohol or drugs, is suicidal, or circumstances are such that a therapist recommends inpatient care, then inpatient treatment is superior for a number of reasons.

5. What are the advantages of inpatient care in those situations?

The first advantage is that your teen is in a highly structured, safe environment, with staff who are trained to recognize a teen's potential for self-destruction.

The second advantage is that in good adolescent programs, such as those at College Hospital and College Hospital Costa Mesa, treatment is extremely intensive. Teens participate in treatment activities for up to 12 hours a day, so they can make much more rapid progress in regaining control. The entire environment is designed to help them learn to live with rules, to make responsible decisions, to communicate effectively, and to get along with others. A teen in outpatient treatment has up to 110 hours a week to intensify bad habits, because behavior isn't constantly monitored and because so many unhealthy choices are available. In an inpatient program there are 110 hours a week to learn new habits, because behavior is closely monitored, because the behavior that is expected is made very clear, and because unhealthy choices, such as drugs, violence, and sex are not available.

6. How can I tell if a hospital program is good?

There are several points to look at. Do the medical and program directors have solid professional reputations? Is there a specialized treatment program for adolescents that is separate from the program for adults? Are there distinct programs or tracks for groups of teens with different kinds of problems? At College Hospital and College Hospital Costa Mesa, for example, there are adolescent programs for out-of-control teens and programs for withdrawn, depressed, or overly-compliant teens. The way these programs are structured is quite different. In addition, College Hospital and College Hospital Costa Mesa offer specialized treatment tracks for teens who are chemically dependent and for those who have suffered serious emotional traumas, such as sexual abuse, violence, or loss of a loved one.

When considering a hospital program, you have a right, even an obligation, to ask questions about the treatment provided. What kind of evaluation does the teen get? Is an individualized treatment plan developed for each teen? Who participates in developing the treatment plan? Is there a certified school program built into the treatment program? What treatment components are provided for family members? Who participates in discharge planning? Is there a partial hospitalization program associated with the treatment program, so the teen can make an effective transition from hospital to home life at the end of inpatient treatment?

Any hospital you consider should give you satisfactory answers to these questions.

7. I don't know anything about mental health treatment. How can I tell if a hospital offers good programs? I'm just a mom.

(1) First inquire whether the hospital is accredited by the Joint Commission on Accreditation of Hospitals. The Joint Commission on Accreditation of Hospitals inspects each member hospital once per year to ensure the highest possible quality of patient care.

(2) But you don't have to be a professional. You can gain a lot of information by reading and asking questions. Ask for program brochures which explain the hospital's programs and treatment philosophy. Before you admit your teen to any inpatient program, you should be able to tour the hospital and meet with the staff. During that time, you can get a sense of the quality of the program. Is the unit clean? Is the staff busy working with patients or sitting around chatting? Do the patients seem to be in control of themselves? Does the program seem well-organized?

8. It seems to me that the success of treatment would pretty much depend upon the initial evaluation. What should the evaluation include?

The evaluation should include a complete psycho-social history. A psycho-social history is an extremely detailed interview of the parents and adolescent, individually, which obtains a complete and thorough background to help the treatment team understand the problem in detail. Psychological testing, a medical history, and a physical examination, which includes a chest x-ray and laboratory work, are also done. An educational history and educational testing should also be included. At College Hospital and College Hospital Costa Mesa, a speech and language screening is also given to every adolescent patient, since it has been found that many teens with emotional and behavioral problems also have learning disabilities that have not been identified by the school.

9. What is an individualized treatment plan?

This is the map that charts your teen's treatment needs. After all evaluation steps have been completed, the treatment team should meet to identify all the problem areas, define specific goals the teen must work toward, and develop specific treatment approaches to help reach those goals. For example, if a teen has problems controlling his temper, one of his treatment goals should be to learn alternatives for lashing out, and his treatment plan should include specific methods to help him learn specific skills that he can use in various situations.

Another example is if the teenager has a problem with alcohol, one of his treatment goals should be to learn the underlying causes for using alcohol. His treatment plan should include specific methods to help him cope with problems that do not involve alcohol.

10. Who should develop the treatment plan?

Treatment planning should be done by every discipline within the treatment team. This includes the psychiatrist, the therapist, the nursing staff, the rehabilitation therapy staff, the social worker, and the educational staff. At College Hospital and College Hospital Costa Mesa, a speech and language pathologist and the dietician also participate in treatment planning, because they are integral parts of the treatment team and have completed evaluations of each teen.

11. My fifteen-year-old is already way below grade level in school. If he goes to an inpatient program for three or four months, won't that just mess up his education that much worse?

Any good treatment program for teens should have a comprehensive, certified educational program built into it. At College Hospital and College Hospital Costa Mesa, for example, teens spend about four hours each day in on-campus classrooms run by teachers who are credentialed in special education. An educational assessment is included in each teen's evaluation, so the educational staff knows each student's strengths and weaknesses. Each teen receives individual attention that can increase academic skills.

12. Do inpatient programs give kids tutoring?

One of the reasons out-of-control kids do so poorly in school is that they can't get along within a classroom. They don't know how to pay attention or keep their mouths shut. Some have such bad classroom skills that they regularly get kicked out of class. If the treatment program just gives them tutoring, they may learn to do well on a one-to-one tutoring basis, but when they leave the hospital and go back to their regular school, they still don't know how to get along in the classroom. College Hospital's and College Hospital Costa Mesa's school programs give individual attention, but it's done within classroom settings, which are a lot more like real life.

The vast majority of teens with emotional and behavioral problems have terrible study habits. If they are ever to do well in school, they have to learn good study skills. At College Hospital and College Hospital Costa Mesa, the school programs have a specialized school component called the Practice Classroom, where the students learn how to pay attention in the classroom, take notes, organize their study time, use reference materials, organize and write reports, and so on. The whole focus of the Practice Classroom is to teach kids how to be students, so when they go back to their home school district, they've got a better chance of keeping up with their grade level.

Often teenagers can improve their grade level half a year or more because of the intensity of the practice classroom in reading, spelling, history, math, and so forth.

13. My nephew was in a psych program and seemed to make a lot of progress in school there. But when he went back to his regular high school, his grades began to slip again. It didn't seem that there was any communication between the treatment program and his school. Is that pretty standard?

It doesn't have to be. Some treatment programs have a good history of working with the student's home school district, so the educational progress the kid makes while in the hospital can be continued after he leaves. When you're checking out inpatient treatment programs, you should ask about how the staff communicates with the school district. Do they recommend individualized educational programs? Do they advocate for the student? Or do they just send the kid back to his regular school and hope for the best?

14. Our daughter has been getting more and more out of control, and I also think she's using drugs. Her behavior is affecting the whole family. If we take her to a hospital will they help us, too, or just her?

They should help the whole family. A good inpatient program for teens recognizes the special problems of the entire family and offers a variety of family treatment components.

Again, because I hospitalize my patients at College Hospital and College Hospital Costa Mesa, I can tell you what they do. Each week they provide parent group therapy, multi-family therapy group, and parenting skills groups.

Parent group therapy consists of the parents meeting without their adolescents to help them understand how to deal with and help their own teenager. Multi-family therapy group is where several families, patients, and parents meet together for therapy. Parenting skills group are where parents learn specific techniques for dealing with their kids.

College Hospital and College Hospital Costa Mesa also provide a teen and sibling group, where several patients and their brothers and sisters work together in therapy. Most hospitals don't offer any treatment components for siblings, but I think it's very important. After all, aren't your other children deeply affected by the behavior and problems of the troubled one? They need help, too.

15. What do kids do in an inpatient program all day? I mean, how do you fill up twelve or fourteen hours a day with therapy?

It's really very easy in comprehensive treatment programs like the ones at College Hospital and College Hospital Costa Mesa. First, there's about four hours in the classroom every day, plus an hour or two of supervised study hall. The kids also participate in a wide variety of therapy groups. Some of them are traditional psychotherapy groups, where they learn to identify and express their feelings in appropriate ways. Psycho-drama is also offered at College Hospital, College Hospital Costa Mesa, and at many other hospitals. Psycho-drama involves parents and adolescents "playing roles" such as a mom and dad, which helps adolescents see the mom's and dad's point of view.

A good program also provides therapy groups that help kids learn important living skills such as communicating with peers, assertiveness, planning constructive leisure time, relaxation, biofeedback, and social skills.

Other treatment groups focus on helping the kids clarify their values and make responsible decisions. These groups include drug and alcohol awareness, sex education, and general value groups.

Life management groups help the teens make decisions about future schooling and jobs and give them skills for handling college or job applications, interviewing, time management, money management, and consumer issues.

Some of the teens in the program also need to learn more basic living skills such as grooming, nutrition, and personal finance, so they'll be better equipped to succeed in independent living.

Then too, if a teen has a problem with alcohol or drugs, part of his treatment should focus specifically on learning about addictions and achieving and maintaining sobriety. Those teen's whose problems are associated with having been victimized participate in specialized groups that help them learn how to feel safer and how to protect themselves from further victimization.

Because the family is still central to a teen's life, his treatment should also include family communication groups, family therapy, and sibling groups.

And because physical health is so closely linked to mental health, some time each day is devoted to physical fitness activities and health education.

Recreational activities, including sports, games, and outings, are also an important part of the teen's treatment activities. Finally, a critical part of the whole inpatient experience is the opportunity to spend time focusing on living together in a community, planning recreational activities, working out disagreements, helping each other, and so on.

Actually, the problem in a good hospital program never seems to be too much time, but rather too little time to effectively address all aspects of a teen's developmental needs.

16. When a teen is ready to leave the inpatient program, what kind of support are he and his family given?

That depends upon the hospital where your teen is treated. Some, unfortunately, don't offer a lot of after-care service. They leave it up to the primary therapist to see the patient, and probably his family, on an outpatient basis for a few months.

Others have a stronger commitment to helping the patient make the transition back into his family, school and community, and to helping the family reintegrate the patient back into family life. They may offer continuing multi-family therapy groups and parenting skills groups to families after the patient has been discharged.

A very small minority of adolescent hospital programs offer intensive transition programs to help the teen reintegrate back into his family and community life. College Hospital, for example, has a Partial Hospitalization Program (PHP). This is basically a day treatment service. Those teens who have been in the inpatient program and are likely to have difficulties in school and family life when they leave the hospital are referred to the PHP. They participate in a special school and treatment program in the daytime but go home every evening and weekend to live with their families. This gives them a chance to practice their new skills at home and with their friends, but they still have the intensive support of the treatment team to help them work out problems. College Hospital's PHP also includes family treatment components, so the parents, and even the siblings, can work with the staff to continue learning new skills for helping the teen. This program has been extremely successful in helping teens and their families make the transition to successful functioning outside of treatment.

17. My sister in the Midwest had her son in a psych hospital for a few months, and she sometimes had a hard time getting some of her questions answered. She was basically happy

with the treatment her son was getting, but sometimes when she wanted information about things, she felt like she was getting the run-around. Where can parents turn in this situation?

It can be frustrating, because there are so many people involved in your teen's treatment program, and different staff members are responsible for different aspects of the treatment. It is difficult to know who to ask about this or that. I would recommend this: if your question is about your teen's problems or his specific treatment, direct your questions to your teen's primary therapist. If the question is about hospital policy or procedure, such as what kind of clothes your teen can wear or whether you can bring him his guitar, ask the head nurse on the treatment unit. If they don't have the answer, ask them to direct you to the staff member who does. If you aren't satisfied, you can go to the Program Director or even to the hospital's Administrator or Medical Director. While they may not have the specific information you want, they can either direct you to the right source or get the answer for you. If the question is important to you, it should be important to them. You have a right to expect the hospital staff and administration to be responsive to your needs. You've entrusted them to help you and your family during a time of crisis, and you have a right to expect them to meet your needs with a respectful and caring attitude.

CHAPTER SIXTEEN

Responsibility

Clarifying the responsibilities of teenagers is crucial if they are to develop and mature. Here are some thoughts in answer to questions parents often ask.

Questions:

1. My son's friends always want him to do things and he forgets his own responsibilities and chores. What should I do?

The first responsibility a teenager has is to work up to his capacity in school. If he is not doing that, you need to set a limit on how much time he can spend with his friends, and insist that he finish his schoolwork and work up to his capacity. Secondly, you need to insist he finish his chores and have them done on time before he can go out with his friends.

2. Should teenagers be allowed to control their own money from a job?

Your responsibility as a parent is to help educate your children about money. First of all, money your teen has earned from a job is his own money, but control of it should depend on how well he is doing in school and whether he is wasting all his money on CDs, tapes, or dates. You might just want to let him waste it all for a while to get it out of his system. However, it is important for you to educate your child about a savings account and about saving money for college, a car, or a trade school. To do this, you might even want to set a limit. For example, put 70% of his money in a savings account to save for things which are important for him, and 30% to do with as he wants. It is certainly not good parenting to allow your teenager to take all his money and blow it over a long period. He will never learn responsibility that way.

If you have any suspicions or knowledge that your teenager is using drugs or alcohol, you would want to take all his money away and put it in a savings account for him until he deals with his drug or alcohol problem.

3. *Our teenage daughter is busy with school and many other activities. We have not asked her to do any chores since she does not have enough time. Is this OK?*

Every member of the family should do some chores. You can vary the amount depending on how busy she is, but I believe chores teach a teenager responsibility, that she has a responsibility to the family, and that everyone does chores. In the summer when she is not so busy, I would certainly increase her chores.

4. *Do you think teenagers should have a part-time job?*

The primary responsibility of a teenager is to go to school and work up to capacity in school. If the teenager is working up to capacity and wants to have a job, that is great. A part-time job is also beneficial in that the single major difference between kids who do well and kids who get into trouble is that those who do well keep very busy. They are busy with jobs, sports, activities, hobbies, and interests.

It can be very rewarding for teenagers to have a part-time job. It teaches them responsibility and the value of money. I would encourage it, but I would not force it.

5. *My ten and eleven-year-olds have to clean the table and set the dishes by the time we get home. If they do not do it, they blame each other. How should I handle them?*

Put a list of chores on the refrigerator and don't give them the same chores. They can each clean and set the table every other day, so you know which one is responsible if it isn't done.

6. *My nineteen-year-old daughter just lays around the house and will not get a job or go to school. What do I do?*

Tell her she must go to a school or work. If she is not willing to do that, then she must leave. Tell her that she has one month, and if she feels there is something preventing her, you will help her get counseling. If you don't do that, you are contributing to her irresponsibility.

When I give this answer to parents, many look as if I had thrust a dagger into their hearts. But if you give the ultimatum and don't enforce it, you are not doing her any good either.

CHAPTER SEVENTEEN

Sex

Of all problems, sex is one area in which teenagers are most vulnerable to anxiety and misfortune. Parents need to learn how to deal with this area to make sure their teenagers don't get into trouble.

Questions:

l. My seventeen-year-old daughter wants to go to family planning for birth control. I don't want to take her because I think she will take it to mean I approve. But I am also concerned that she may get pregnant because she has a new boyfriend. What can I do?

Many years ago, I stopped being anything but pragmatic in my approach to adolescents and sex. My approach is to deal with the reality of the l980's and '90's; it is a psychological approach, not a moral or religious approach.

We see too many teenage girls who are pregnant. It is almost always a disaster for them and their family. I have not seen, in seventeen years of specializing in working with adolescents, any seventeen, eighteen or nineteen-year-old girls whom I consider mature enough to be responsible and good parents.

Being pregnant and having a child when you are an immature teen creates severe psychological problems for the child. The young mother often bitterly resents the child because she feels she must spend time with it and nurture it, instead of doing things which are appropriate for kids her age. It also becomes a major economic problem, since teenagers cannot get good enough jobs to live on their own and take care of a child. Most often, they do not marry the father, and he does not contribute any financial support. Often the mother becomes dependent on her own parents, which creates even more resentment, as the grandparents of the child have to be involved both financially and emotionally, almost becoming the child's parents.

If the girl has the baby and gives it up for adoption, there are psychological scars. If she has an abortion, there are also psychological scars and possibly physiological consequences for having children in the future.

My answer for you is to take your daughter to the family planning center. Let her know, though, that it does not mean you approve, but that you are certainly willing to help once she has made a decision to get contraceptives, because you care about her and don't want her to ruin her life getting pregnant.

2. What do you do with a seventeen-year-old girl who is sexually active with a number of different guys? She has had an abortion already. How do you redirect her so she stops having sex?

If she has been sexually active for a number of years, you are certainly not going to get her to stop having sexual relationships with a number of guys immediately.

The first thing to do is make sure she is using birth control.

Teenagers who are sexually active with more than one partner almost always have extremely poor self-esteem. They are trying to get popularity or acceptance by giving themselves to others. Ultimately, they will wind up being used time and time again. But since they feel so strongly that they have nothing to offer (because of their tremendously low self-esteem), they continue to follow the pattern of having sex with more than one person.

Without being aware of it, some teenage girls attempt to become pregnant. What they are trying to do unconsciously is to reaffirm their femininity by proving they can have a child.

Also, for many teenage girls having sex makes them feel like an adult.

I would immediately get her to counseling and have the therapist deal with the self-esteem problem.

3. What do you tell ten and eleven-year-olds when they start talking about sex and start asking questions?

I don't think there are any parents out there who would not wish that teenagers would abstain from sex until they are married.

Every year one million teenage girls become pregnant, and as I indicated in the question above, it is often a disaster for them and everyone else involved. Again, my answer is a pragmatic one which has nothing to do with religious or moral beliefs; it has to do with what I call "the reality of the '80's and '90's."

Since only 25% of teenage girls who have sex use birth control, you can, as a parent, educate your adolescents in birth control, while also letting them know what your values are. It is also important to let them know that they are going to make the decision, and while you may not approve of their decision, you want to know about it. Their decision won't affect how you feel about them, but you insist that they act responsibly if they decide to have sex, and that means using birth control.

4. What can you do for a twelve or thirteen-year-old to make sure she does not have sex until she is married?

There is nothing I can say which will give you any sort of guarantee.

What I can tell you is that there is a strong correlation between poor self-esteem and how early kids get sexually involved. Those who get sexually involved later on have a much higher self-esteem. If you want to do anything, I would focus in the area of self-esteem. I would give your children many compliments, spend time with them, and make sure the doors of communication are open. You can also do everything possible to make sure your children do well in school and are involved in activities, hobbies, or interests.

I cannot emphasize enough the significance of having a high self-esteem. Such teenagers are far less likely to become involved in things which are no good for them.

> THEME THREE:
> What To Do If You're Having Lots Of Problems
> With Your Teen

CHAPTER EIGHTEEN

Rebellion

When there are lots of problems with teenagers, many parents simply do not know what to do with age-appropriate rebellion and inappropriate rebellion. This area is often quite alarming for parents. Lets look at this problem.

QUESTIONS:

1. Is a teenager's room her own domain, or should parents be allowed to force teenagers to clean up if it is so messy no one can walk through?

A messy room is a very safe form of rebellion compared to other things. Parents do have the right to ask that things be reasonably clean. There should certainly not be any odors, garbage, or food. You could put a little pressure on your teenager to clean up, but do not force the issue, because if you clamp down too hard she might resort to unsafe ways to rebel. If you do not say anything about it, she may figure it does not irritate you and then it loses its effectiveness as a rebellion.

2. How do you draw the line for a fourteen-year-old boy between back talk and verbal abuse as a safe form of rebellion?

First, you never let the kid swear at you. Second, you never let your kid call you a name, like dumb or stupid. You may allow him to state that your behavior is stupid, but not that you are. Then, depending on your own comfort level as a parent, you could let him raise his voice and yell during an argument or disagreement.

Some parents may find that intolerable, so just say you will not accept yelling.

About back talk, there is no rule saying that parents have to tolerate this. So, if you have had a bad day at work and do not want to argue with your teenager, say, "I have heard your side of the story and here is my position. This ends the discussion. If you continue arguing you will be punished." If you want to talk about it more, that is fine also; but again, you have the right to limit the amount of back talk you will take.

3. Aren't adolescents set with their habits by seventeen, so if they are messy, they will stay that way for life?

No. They are still going through rebellion. The rebellion can last as long as twenty-three to twenty-five. So there is a chance that sometime, probably when they are out of your house, they could be neat.

4. My teenager does well in all areas except that he writes pornographic letters to friends. Is this abnormal?

This could be a sign of a serious problem. Take him to a therapist to get it checked out.

5. My daughter just started acting in unacceptable ways, such as back talking and not doing chores.

Statistically, most kids start rebelling somewhere between ten and thirteen. This is unusual, but it is still age-appropriate, and you can be glad she is rebelling in safe ways as opposed to unsafe ways. The alternative is that she could rebel much more severely later on, in ways which are almost always unsafe. The other alternative, as I mentioned earlier, is that somewhere between nineteen and twenty-five, kids who do not rebel can get very depressed and often suicidal.

6. How do you handle a teenager who always has to have the last word?

While the definition of safe rebellion is some behavior which is guaranteed to have your stomach in a knot most of the time, it is not harmful to either of you. Let him have the last word—so what? It is a safe form of rebellion.

7. My eleven-year-old has a bad attitude problem, and whenever I tell her to do something, she looks as if she were having a seizure. Her eyes roll back, her head goes back and she looks like she'd kill me. What do I do?

This is a safe form of rebellion. Let her do all those things. If what you describe is the worst thing she does in adolescence, consider yourself fortunate.

8. When do kids grow out of this rebellious stage?

There is good news and bad news. The good news is that they grow out of it; the bad news is it can be as late as twenty-two to twenty-five.

9. Can I punish safe forms of rebellion which irritate me all the time? For example, our son does not care how loud he plays his music and it bothers everyone else in the family, or he takes all the cans of Coke and does not leave any for anyone else.

Yes, those are safe forms of rebellion. But you do not have to let him walk all over you. Simply tell him, "Turn the music down or off, because it is bothering me and other members of the family. I do not want loud music when I am relaxing, watching TV or reading the paper."

You can also tell him, "There are six cans of coke in the refrigerator. You may have one or two for the day, but if you take more, you will be punished." Then go ahead and punish if you need to.

10. I am a devout Christian and believe my teenager should pray every night and go to church, but he refuses to. What can I do?

There are two parts to your question. One is psychological and one is theological. I cannot answer the theological part since it is not my field of expertise. My expertise is in the field of psychotherapy.

From a psychological point of view, not praying with you every night or going to church every week is a safe form of rebellion. Again, the definition of a safe form of rebellion is a behavior which puts your stomach in knots all the time. What I have seen happen is that parents will force their teenager to go to church or synagogue, and such hatred will build up that he will not come back to it when he is older or an adult.

The theological part of the question seems to come from the fact you feel so strongly that your son is missing his spiritual life. I suggest that you consult your minister, because I am not qualified to answer that issue.

Another option for you to consider is trying to make a compromise with your son. Perhaps he will agree to going to church every other week.

11. I am afraid for my daughter because everytime we have a disagreement, she disappears into her room for hours at a time. It hurts me that she is so unhappy. What should I do?

This is a safe form of rebellion, and you should not get worried if your daughter is unhappy when you are doing your job as a parent. She may be using that as manipulation, so don't give in. There is no problem if she wants to sulk and act immature, or just wants some time to herself.

12. My twelve-year-old girl wants to wear everything black, a lot of makeup, including lipstick, eye makeup and blush. Should I stop her?

With a twelve-year-old girl, I would suggest you severely limit the makeup, and I would not allow her to wear all black because that often leads to becoming involved with the punk scene.

13. My thirteen-year-old daughter and her two friends share makeup and clothes all the time. My husband won't allow it and becomes angry because he thinks it is not hygenic, especially when they exchange underwear and swimsuits. We are having a war in our house. What do you suggest?

Again, since this bothers your husband so much, it is obviously a safe form of her rebellion. I would not make a war out of this. You could insist that your daughter wash the underwear and swimsuits before wearing them. But you should count your blessings that she is not rebelling with drugs or in other dangerous ways.

14. My fourteen-year-old daughter slams doors all the time when she is angry. Is this a safe form of rebellion?

In almost all cases where an adolescent slams doors there is a parent who also slams doors when he is angry. I do not believe that your teenager should be allowed to hit the door or kick it. But door slamming to me is a pretty safe form of rebellion. If anything gets damaged, though, she should pay for it.

15. Whenever our sixteen-year-old son is mad, he leaves the house and walks around for half hour or so and then he comes back when he is calm. Is that a safe form of rebellion?

Yes. I would make an agreement with him that he is not to drive the car when he is angry, and he needs to be within a ten minute walk of the house, and yes, that is a safe form of rebellion.

16. My fifteen-year-old daughter spends her life on the phone. What is the best way to get her off it?

Monopolizing the phone is a very safe form of rebellion. If she is working up to her capacity in school, getting along reasonably well with you as parents, doing her chores, and has a good peer group, then I would not worry. Let her talk all she wants and set limits for it if you need to use it. But if she is not doing well in school or doesn't do her chores, limit her phone privileges more severely until they improve.

CHAPTER NINETEEN

School and School Problems

The adolescent's fundamental task or "job" is to go to school and to work to the highest level that he can in each subject. For example, if a teenager can get a "B" in English and he is working up to his capacity, that is great. If he can get a "D+" in algebra and he is working up to his capacity in that subject, that is great, as well. There is a real strong correlation between how well people do in school and how well they do in later life.

School teaches adolescents study habits, discipline, time management, how to get along with their peers, and how to get along with authority figures.

Your responsibility as a parent is to make sure your youngster works up to his capacity in every subject in school. This chapter is designed to help you do that.

Our society places a tremendous importance and a high value on going to school, doing well, and getting an education. Whether this is right or wrong is not the point as much as it is a fact of life. Kids who do well in school, generally speaking, have good self-esteem, and those who do not usually have low self-esteem.

Kids who do below average, poor, or badly in school almost always have poor self-esteem since others often judge them according to their achievements.

Questions:

1. I help my teenager two hours a night with math, but he is not turning it in to his class. What can I do?

This is a very self-defeating pattern, to do homework and not turn it in. You might point this out to him, and explain that he has a responsibility to turn in his homework. Then tell him if he does not turn in his homework, you will render the consequences. You should also see whether this self-defeating pattern occurs in any other areas of his life.

If this is true, counseling is certainly in order, especially if his behavior doesn't change after the consequences.

2. How do you get a teenager to go to school? My seventeen-year-old son has not gone to school for a year and a half.

The teenager is out of control and running the show. You need to do everything you can to get back into control. If he has been out of school for a year and a half, you might not want to start with school but instead sit down with him and say, "Look, you will have to do something constructive; work full time, go to night school, trade school, or continuation school, and you have a week to decide and start." Then do whatever you must to get him to do what he has chosen which is acceptable to you. Also, see the chapter on "Out Of Control."

3. My daughter is changing schools. She is going to junior high and I want to know how I can help her make that transition.

Here are some suggestions: l. Before junior high starts, take her to the school so she sees what it looks like and becomes familiar with it. 2. Go with her when she enrolls, even if it means taking off work. 3. Acknowledge what she is feeling and say something like, "I know it is scary for you to go from a place where you knew most of the people and had many friends to a new place where you do not know anyone. It is very difficult, and anytime you want to talk about it let me know; I am available." 4. Besides acknowledging how tough it is, offer to help her get new friends, encouraging her to invite kids over, go to activities, or invite someone to a movie. Tell her you will help with driving, and do all you can to help her make new friends.

4. What do you do with a kid who is capable of getting all "A's" but is getting "C's" and "D's," grades which are apparently going down more each quarter?

I suggest that you give your teen a little lecture, saying, "Look, there is a strong correlation between how well you do in school and how well you will do later in life. School teaches you time management, discipline, study habits, and how to get along with adult supervisors and a wide variety of peers. My responsibility to you, as your parent, is to make sure you work up to capacity."

Then institute a progress report. All school districts in Southern California have these. If you are not from Southern California, you might want to check and see what your own school district has. The progress report works like this: you call your school counselor and ask that your kid be put on a progress report. Then every Friday, he brings home a paper stating how well he has done in each class that week, whether he has turned his homework in, and if his citizenship has been satisfactory. If the report shows anything unacceptable, you ground him or take away a privilege for the weekend.

Do not accept any excuses for not bringing home the progress report. If the excuse is that the substitute teacher would not sign it, or he lost it, consequences are to be rendered. Keep doing this and raising the consequences until his grades are up to his capacity.

5. What if you institute a progress report and it does not work?

Then sit down with your teenager and say, "Look, you choose an hour which is good for you, whether it is 5:30 to 6:30, 7:30, etc., and it will be study hall for you. I am going to keep an eye on you while you study. If you need my help and I can help, I will be glad to, but you are going to study and do whatever it takes to get you up to your grade capacity."

6. What do you do if your teen tells you she is really confused about homework, and just does not want to do it?

Often adolescents are confused and do not know what they think or feel. They are going through puberty, changing schools, and making new friends. This often happens so fast it can be confusing and upsetting. You can outline the behavior you expect of them during this period, which will give them the guidelines they need. When they do not have guidelines, and run into problems while lacking the ability to express their feelings, they often signal us with their behavior.

An adolescent who is not doing well in school is signaling us with her behavior that she is unhappy and has a problem. This behavior is even more significant if she has problems in other areas of her life. You might talk with her about what other parts of her life are unhappy? How does she get along with friends? How is she getting along with her parents? Does she have any drug or alcohol problems? For the school problem alone I recommend counseling.

7. What do you do with a seventeen-year-old who is not motivated by school, and wants to sit around all summer driving his mother nuts? Does the mother have the right to tell him to get a job?

Absolutely. I suggest telling him he must do something acceptable to you. Whether it is taking some trade classes in a school program, going to summer school or getting a job, it does not matter, but it must be something which is acceptable, since you will not allow him to sit around all summer.

8. What if he will not do any of those and refuses to get a job, or says he is looking for a job but cannot find one?

Get him jobs around the neighborhood. Volunteer him to cut other peoples' lawns, clean up their trash, and other things which will motivate him to find his own job.

9. I have been listening to what you say and am disappointed in my parenting, since we have always allowed our kids to get just "C's" when they are capable of getting "B's" and "A's." But how do we change?

Sit down with your kids and explain to them why you expect them to work up to their ability (see other questions for an explanation). Tell them your expectations, and that if they do not meet them, there will be consequences. You are going to measure their progress by progress reports. For example, if they are getting "C's" for three quarters, an "A" may be out of reach, but not a "B." Follow the progress reports to see what they get the last quarter, and if their progress reports are not satisfactory, give them consequences, being strict and firm.

10. My fifteen-year-old has been going with a girl for years. Now he is talking about getting married and finding a job. His performance in school has dropped, as well. What should I do? I am so angry at the girl I will not let her come around.

Tell him you are going to limit the amount of time he spends with the girl until his grades are up to what he is capable of achieving, and do everything you can to enforce it.

You might also try to remedy the situation with the girl by allowing her to come to your house, so that you will at least know where they both are at that time.

11. Every time our daughter, a sophomore in college, gets

angry at us, she threatens to drop out because all of her friends are making more money working, and she is attracted by that.

Tell her there is a new rule in your house. She is not to threaten you about quitting college when she is angry. That kind of behavior will not be accepted. If she wants to quit college, you can all sit down and talk about it, but she can not use it as a threat.

You might point out options by saying, "It is very attractive to have a lot of money, work full time, buy a new car, and go to Palm Springs with your friends. However, kids who go to college and get their degree almost always do better in the long run."

If she does eventually quit college and works for a while, it is not the end of the world. Kids her age need to test and try out different options. She can always return to college.

Sometimes kids just have to learn things the hard way.

12. *My seventeen-year-old son, who is mentally gifted and used to get "A's" is now going downhill fast. He is getting "F's," wants to drop out of school, and comes home drunk. He yells at me often, and I am afraid he is going to hit me. What can I do?*

You are seeing a clear pattern of self-destructive behavior in all the major areas of his life. In school, he is going downhill, he wants to drop out, he has an alcohol problem, yells and swears at his mother, and is getting very violent.

With this behavior, you are not just seeing a school problem but one which involves his whole life. It is severe enough to recommend counseling immediately.

13. *What do you do with a child who will not do his homework on a regular basis? He is eleven and does it whenever he feels like it.*

Set him up on a study program at any time which is convenient for your family, whether it is at 6:00, 7:00 or 8:00, etc. You find out what his homework is and monitor it. If he does not finish it, punish him. Then you request weekly progress reports. If he does not work up to his grade level, you punish him more. You keep escalating the punishment until you get back into control.

14. *What would you do with a nineteen-year-old who dropped out of high school and still is not working after two months?*

Give her a choice of either getting a full time job, enrolling again in school, or going to trade school. Tell her she has a month to begin one of the choices or she will have to leave the home.

15. Is independent study a good thing if your teenager does not want to go to school?

As a rule, no, for a number of reasons: 1. It is so easy it becomes a joke. Teens can, in most programs, do a full week's school work in two or three hours. 2. Very few kids have the internal motivation to do it. 3. If you are not at home, it is an open invitation for him to "get away with murder." 4. If you are at home, the independent study might take him all of 45 minutes a day to do, and then he is left with nothing constructive to do all day.

Other things you might consider are the Regional Occupational Program (ROP), which is a work-study program after school, or night school.

In the ROP, the teen would go to school in the morning and then choose an ROP work class in the afternoon.

16. My fourteen-year-old daughter's school had a "back to school night," for which I was all excited to go. My daughter said it was really stupid for me to go, and was really against my going.

I always encourage parents to be involved as much as possible and go to "back to school nights." Teens may think them silly or dumb, and may be embarrassed if their parents go. This is usually normal. Another explanation for this behavior is that there may be something she did not want you to find out from the teacher. Just simply say to her, "Hey, I am going to parent's night because I am concerned about you, and want to meet your teacher and visit your classes."

17. I have already instituted a progress report and given consequences, but my son still is not doing well in school. He says he has no homework and will not bring his books home.

You can tell if he is lying by monitoring the progress report. If he does not bring them home, you punish him. You keep escalating the consequences until you get back into control and he does what he is capable of in school. You also establish a study hall and sit down with him to monitor his homework.

19. Every time we try to get our daughter started on homework, it is World War III. She fights, screams, and hollers. We go through half an hour of this before she sits down and does some homework.

Tell her there is a new rule in your house. She must do homework when you tell her. Set a time for a study hall and say, "If you do not start it without all this fighting and hassling, there will be consequences. I am not willing to go through a war with you every night when it is time to do your homework."

20. What do you do with a kid who is in sixth grade, getting very bad grades, says he does not like school, none of his friends like school, and that it is all stupid?

Tell him he is entitled to his feelings, but he is going to work up to his grade level in school. If he does not, he will receive consequences. Then you go ahead and give the punishment.

21. What if your teenager cuts school for just one day?

If your teenager cuts school for a day, punish the teen by taking away a privilege for one evening. Say it is not acceptable in your home to cut school, and that there is a punishment for this type of behavior. If you do it again, the punishment will be much worse.

22. What is the best approach to change a twelve-year-old who is doing poorly in junior high, getting "D's" and "F's," and blames it on the teacher? He did fine during fifth grade, but now in sixth grade he is having a lot of problems.

It is common for kids to do well in grammar school and have a sudden drop-off when they go to junior high or high school. The first thing to do is put your son on a progress report and punish him unless he works up to his capacity. If he has a conflict with the teacher, then you can try to understand his side, meet with the teacher and try to get things solved. But he is going to do homework, and will be punished if he doesn't do it and raise his grades.

23. What if your teenager has a lot of ability but just does enough to get by?

You explain to her how important school is (see the previous answers in this chapter), tell her what you expect, put her on a progress report, and punish her if she does not get the grades she is capable of getting.

24. How do you get an adolescent to want to do homework on his own, and sit down to do it every day?

Generally speaking, there are two types of motivation: internal and external. What you want is to get your son internally motivated, while it appears he is only externally motivated. You need to structure external motivation so eventually there will be internal motivation. External motivation includes things such as progress reports, study halls, and punishment, which you combine with explanations on the importance of school in order to turn it into internal motivation.

25. How do you motivate a teenager to do well in school?

Sit down with her and explain that as an adult, your basic task is to go to work, and the teenager's basic job is to go to school, working up to the highest possible level she is capable. (Also use some of the other material from this chapter). Tell her, "It is our responsibility and obligation to get you to work to the best of your ability." Then put her on a progress report and punish her if she does not bring her grades up to an acceptable level.

26. What if my teenager is out of control and won't go to school at all; he takes off in the morning and just hangs around the beach or with his friends?

Tell him he is out of control and you will do everything possible to get him back into control. The first time he is absent again, take everything out of his room except the mattress and a couple changes of clothes. Lock everything else in your garage or your neighbor's. Tell him this is just the beginning and you will go up from there. Do everything you have to in order to get back in control.

27. The school called saying my son has not been in his classes for thirty-six days. His grades have gone to "D's" and "F's" while he surfs all day. What can I do?

You take the surfboard and all the equipment away and lock it up somewhere. Then say, "This stops! You are going to school, and cannot surf until you stay in school and raise your grades. We will do whatever we must to get you to go to school and make this happen."

28. What do you do with a twenty-year-old who is just going to college to avoid work? She takes gym classes and other easy ones like photography and shop class without ever getting better than "C's" or caring about it.

Tell her that unless she takes classes of which you approve, you will not support her going to college, so she will either have to work or leave home.

29. I am doing much of what you suggest with the school work, but it is still a day-to-day battle to get my teen to do it. Sometimes he is better than others, and I think, eventually, I will succeed. But most of the time, I feel I am the one being

punished, since it is so draining, frustrating, and exhausting to deal with him. What do I do?

You can relieve your frustration by talking about how angry you are to your husband, friends, or others in your support system. It is important that you don't keep it bottled up inside. It is fine to acknowledge to yourself the times you may have hated your kid, wished he were never born, that he would run away, or that you could run away. All parents have these feelings at one time or another if they are honest with themselves. It is just part of the price you pay for being a parent.

CHAPTER TWENTY

Drugs and Alcohol

My position on drug or alcohol usage is very clear: unequivocally, no drug or alcohol usage is acceptable. Drug and alcohol usage is extremely damaging to an adolescent physically and psychologically.

There is a drug and alcohol epidemic among our youth that has been unprecedented in our history.

In nationwide polls, our teenagers have admitted that the majority of them have tried their first drug at thirteen and alcohol at twelve. It is no wonder that there are now 3.3 million teenage alcoholics and 2.7 million teenage drug addicts. One third of all high school seniors get drunk at least once a week. One out of six seniors has tried cocaine or crack. High school girls take more stimulants and tranquilizers than boys, almost matching their alcohol usage. Even one third of fourth graders have already been pressured by their peers to try alcohol and marijuana. These statistics are frightening. But drug and alcohol usage is almost always an indication of an underlying problem. Here are some things to look for in your adolescent's behavior that could indicate that there is a drug or alcohol problem: when your teenager's school grades drop, they lose interest in their physical appearance or health, their peer group changes dramatically, they display a sudden lack of motivation, or they become extremely secretive.

When a teenager is using drugs or alcohol, the parents are almost always the last to know. A poll of six hundred teens and parents by Emory University in Atlanta revealed that only 35% of the parents believed their teen had had some kind of alcohol in the past month, while their children admitted it was actually twice that number. The same is true of marijuana, where most parents said it was a problem, but only 20% believed their kids were involved. When in reality, over 50% of the teens had tried it, and one-third were using it regularly.

Our experience is that even when parents believe or suspect drug usage, their perception of the extent of the usage is usually underestimated by ten. In other words, adolescents use drugs and alcohol a minimum of ten times more frequently than the average parent suspects.

When it comes to your attention that your teenager is involved with drugs or alcohol, act quickly, for it is your teenager's life which is at stake. You should get counseling immediately, and start your teenager on the process of rehabilitation.

Questions:

1. My sixteen-year-old son claims not to use drugs or alcohol, but still insists on going to parties where others do. What shall I do?

I believe he is probably using drugs and alcohol. What usually happens at such parties is that there is no parental supervision, and that teenagers there are involved in drug use and sex. For those kids who may not be doing those things, there is still the factor of peer pressure, which can be very powerful. You must also consider your adolescent's safety, since he may be riding with others who are under the influence of drugs or alcohol. All in all, such activities are a very bad environment for a teenager and should be stopped. As a concerned parent, you should help find alternative activities.

2. How do you know if your kids are using drugs or alcohol?

Look for obvious signs, such as alcohol on the breath or staggering. Many parents are the last to know, because often the signs are subtle. You could also look for a pattern where the teenager's life is deteriorating in one or more areas. Further examples are: going downhill in school, hanging around kids you do not approve of, becoming more and more defiant, cutting school or not going altogether, spending no time with you, staying out late, or secret phone calls that you cannot hear.

3. Once we suspect our teenager is taking drugs or alcohol, how can we know for sure?

By the time most parents have suspected drugs, the actual amount of use by the teenager is usually ten to twenty times more than the parents had thought. Unfortunately, parents seem to be the last to know. The best way to tell for sure if your teenager is using drugs is to take him to your family doctor and get a urine test.

4. *How long do drugs or alcohol stay in the system, and how long after they are taken do you need to go the the laboratory?*

How long it stays in the system depends on the drug, how long the teenager has been using it, and on the size and weight of the person involved. Generally speaking, alcohol leaves the system the fastest, usually within forty-eight hours. The barbiturate class of drugs seems to remain the longest, at least three to four weeks. Probably the best time to take your teenager to a lab for a checkup is the same day you suspect him of using drugs, the day after, or on a Monday. The reason for taking your teenager in on a Monday is that drug usage is more frequent on weekends.

5. *How should I handle my thirteen-year-old son's smoking?*

Do not allow it. Parents have an obligation to interfere when something jeopardizes their child's health, safety and welfare; and nicotine certainly does. Nicotine is addicting, and it is very clear that there is a correlation between smoking and lung cancer and other diseases.

6. *Are drug problems among adolescents increasing?*

We are seeing a leveling off of drug use, but an increase in the amount of alcohol kids are using. Obviously, if your child has an alcohol problem, she will be just that much more susceptible to drug use. Many adolescents use both drugs and alcohol. Also, the longer she has a problem, the harder it is to change; so it is important to treat the problem as soon as possible.

7. *How do you raise a child to ensure he will not have a drug or alcohol problem, when drug use is so prevalent in society and schools today?*

The most important thing you could do as a parent is to build your child's self-esteem. Underlying every teenager with a drug and alcohol problem is a kid with poor self-esteem. So give your kids praise, support, and spend time with them, using the skills outlined in my book, *How To Live With Your Teenager: A Survivor's Handbook For Parents*. These are communication skills which teach you to listen to the feelings behind the words. Using effective parenting skills is the best foundation I know for enabling kids to grow up with good self-esteem, which is the best insurance against your adolescent using drugs.

8. Many parents, including myself, have used marijuana when they were teenagers. *My friends and I who used it in high school regularly have turned out very well, and are now working successfully as CPA's and attorneys. Why then must parents be so wary of any drug use by their adolescents?*

We have over 3.3 million kids with severe alcohol problems, and over 2.7 million kids with severe drug problems, most of whom started with marijuana. We have a major epidemic of drug usage in the country by adults. It costs the country billions of dollars in lost time from work, in treatment of addiction, and in crime by addicts and those who use criminal means to gain money for dope. The drug problem in this country is out of control. Your experience of a small group of high school students who used a lot of marijuana and now are all successful can be compared to a car going l00 miles an hour down a curving, winding, mountain road and not getting into an accident. I believe that you and your friends were lucky. But, if we apply your logic to adolescents, letting them use marijuana regularly, statistically the results will be very tragic. Besides being illegal, what you did was dangerous, since there are clear results of research showing that marijuana has many damaging side effects. From what you said, your regular usage could be defined as an addiction. So if you are telling me you are proud of the fact that you and your friends were addicts, I cannot agree with you.

9. What do you do if you find drugs in your teenager's room?

Don't talk to her when you are upset. Wait until you are calm, however long it takes, then talk to her. You might say, "I was putting your clothes away and I saw this. I am very concerned. Can we talk about it?" Sometimes a teenager will lie and deny it is hers, saying it's a friend's. I do not ever believe that. Again, look for a pattern of deteriorating behavior and immediately get counseling at the first sign of drug use. Patterns that I am very concerned about include a child who is deteriorating or going down in school grades, cutting classes, getting into trouble with teachers in school or not going to school, getting more rebellious and out of control around the home, staying out later at night, and hanging around with friends of whom you don't approve.

If a child does acknowledge using drugs and you want to get a true picture of how much she is using, take whatever she admits to and multiply it by ten to twenty. That is what I have found to be most accurate.

10. How do I know whether my teenager is using drugs or just experimenting?

Something like 75% of kids have tried pot by their junior year of high school. Again, the parent does not know whether it is experimentation or regular usage. The best way to find out is to go to counseling and get a professional evaluation.

11. I know teenagers can get drugs at school from other students, but should parents get involved in trying to stop the drugs at school?

If you know of a certain student who is dealing in school, I would certainly report it to the principal. If you want to get involved in a larger school-wide program, it becomes a political question which I cannot answer for you. Any kid in any junior high school or high school can get just about any drug on any given day. What you need to do as a parent is to use all your resources to make sure it is not your kid using drugs or alcohol.

12. Do you consider any drug use addiction?

No. If an adolescent experiments with pot once or twice, that is not an addiction. Neither is trying it three times a year. However, if any drug or alcohol is used on a regular basis, then it is a problem. A regular basis would be twice a month, once a week, or more often.

13. Could we possibly push our kids into drugs by being lax on the rules at home?

I would say that if your teenager gets away with a lot at home, he is not going to fear any consequences for using drugs. If he has tendencies towards drugs, this parenting style will even accelerate his tendencies.

14. What are the early signs of an involvement in drugs or alcohol? Recently my adolescent daughter has become extremely secretive. Is this a warning sign?

Secretiveness in and of itself is not necessarily an indication of drug usage. Most kids, as they become teenagers, begin to share much less with their parents, spend less time with their parents, and are cautious about talking on the phone when parents are around. But if you suspect drug use, look for patterns in your teen's behavior, such as when grades go down and when the peer group starts to change. See Question 9 for more detailed examples of destructive patterns in your teenager. If you are suspicious, you need to get a urine test done in order to know positively.

15. My teenage daughter says that if I don't let her go to parties, she will lose all her friends. Besides, she says there is nothing else to do.

Before I would let any adolescent go to a party, I would want to know the phone number. I would call to make sure there are parents there, and ask if there are going to be any drugs or alcohol. I would also tell the adolescent that you reserve the right to pop in during the evening to see how things are.

16. What do you think about these teenage bars where they do not serve alcohol?

What kids have told me about them is that drugs are available to be bought and sold in washrooms and in the parking lots. I would not let my kids go to one.

17. How do you know, when your teen goes to a cast party from a play, that someone won't put something in their drink?

I would not allow a kid to go to a cast party if there are no adults, since there will almost always be drinking and alcohol.

18. My seventeen-year-old is starting to rebel more and more. He goes over to another friend's home whose parents allow them to have as much beer as they want.

You tell him that this is not acceptable, and that he cannot go over to the other friend's house, period. You then back up your decision with consequences and do whatever you must to get back into control.

19. My daughter, who is a little immature, states that her friends are very important to her and that she needs to go to their parties in order to have a social life. I know there is drinking and drugs going on, but I do not want to make her stop because then she will have self-esteem problems.

My position is different. You say your daughter is immature and her social life consists of a need to impress the kinds of people who go to parties where there are drugs and alcohol. You would allow her to go? I couldn't disagree more strongly. Do not let her. There will be nothing but problems. She will be tempted and probably use drugs and alcohol, or be involved with kids who are driving under the influence of drugs and alcohol. In many of these types of parties there is a lot of sex going on, as well. Her immaturity could easily lead her into sexual activity.

If she loses these types of friends, it may be the best thing for her.

20. Everytime I ask my son where he is going, there is a war. He says it is none of my business and that I do not trust him.

Tell him that if he wants to leave the house, he has to tell you where he is going and give you a phone number and address. Otherwise he cannot leave. Tell him that it is your responsibility as a parent to check up on him, and you are going to do that. If he does not like it, he can stay home. If you do not trust him, tell him, saying, "Based on this fact, I do not trust you." If you do trust him, tell him it is not an issue of trust, just the way you choose to be a parent.

21. When I tell my sixteen-year-old he cannot hang out with certain friends because they use drugs and alcohol, he does not deny it, but says that I don't trust him. Otherwise, I would know he wouldn't use any.

Tell him that trust is not the issue as much as the temptation to join his friends in using drugs and alcohol. There is a tremendous pressure on kids in such situations, and you should not allow him to be with kids who use drugs or alcohol. Another problem is what happens when they use drugs or alcohol. You do not want him in a car with a driver who uses drugs or alcohol, since often they do stupid things and take chances. Do not allow your son to be with such people, and do whatever you must to keep him in control.

22. My kid works part-time and I am fairly sure he is using drugs. I am concerned that he is using the money from his job to buy the drugs. What can I do? Do I take the money away, or make him quit work?

The first thing you do is make an assessment of whether he is using drugs or not. You can do that by taking him to counseling or by going to your medical doctor and getting a urine test. If you find he is using drugs, get him into counseling. You could work with the counselor from there to deal with the issue of the money and the part-time job. Having the part-time job is very good because it keeps him busy. Almost always, a job helps build self-esteem. You might decide with the counselor that, until he is off drugs, you put the money into a savings account.

23. Is smoking a safe way to rebel?

I consider it an unsafe way to rebel. The Surgeon General says smoking causes lung cancer and all sorts of other problems. It also leads to nicotine addiction.

24. What do you do with two teenagers, sixteen and eighteen, who drink socially probably once or twice a week? They are both doing well in school and in sports, and it doesn't seem to be affecting anything.

I am very much against it. First, if they are drinking socially, and it is not in your house, they still need to get home. So they are either driving under the influence of alcohol, or are with someone who is. Also, they are learning that it is acceptable to use alcohol socially to reduce pressure and stress, and as a way of enjoying life as an adolescent. It is clear that this is how more problems start, that usage only becomes greater, and that at one point it turns into addiction. What I suggest is to do anything to get this drinking to stop.

25. If up to 75% of teenagers experiment with drugs or alcohol, do you think that I should drag my teenager off to a drug rehabilitation program or a psychologist just for experimenting once or twice?

If you could say without a doubt that your kid used them just once or twice, the answer is no. That is clear experimentation. Very few parents can say that though, although most parents want to believe it. Remember, it is always better to be safe than sorry.

When problems arise, it is a human tendency not to want to deal with them. We say, "boys will be boys," or, "they will grow out of it," or that our children's drug usage is only experimentation. As problems such as drug use arise during adolescence, I often tell parents to consider the analogy of going to a dentist for an annual checkup. Why not take your teenager to a counselor for a checkup to avert serious problems later, and for your own peace of mind now? If you suspect any problems in your teenager's life, it is far better to err on the side of caution than to jeopardize your child's health and happiness.

26. My sixteen-year-old is out of control. He is going to counseling, but it does not seem to be working. He still goes to parties every Saturday and comes home drunk, which scares me. What do I do?

If the counseling does not seem to be working, you might get a medical doctor, your family physician, or a school psychologist to recommend another counselor for a second opinion. The length of time your son has been in counseling would make a difference as to whether you should start looking for another counselor. In the meantime, you might tell your son what every parent should consider telling their kids: "If you are ever at a friend's house and are drunk, or the people you are with are drunk, I do not want you driving home. Call me and I will come pick you up. If that is impossible, I want you to spend the night there. If you do this, I promise I will not punish you."

27. How can I, as a parent, enforce a rule for my teenage children about never drinking without seeming hypocritical, since I enjoy drinking myself? What can I say to them?

Ideally, to be a good role model, don't drink at all. Otherwise, explain your position clearly to your teens. Tell them drinking is a serious decision which they can decide upon when they reach legal age. As an adult, you've made the decision to drink alcohol occasionally. However, stress that while you enjoy it, you never misuse it by getting drunk or driving under its influence.

28. Is the same thing true if I smoke?

Smoking any amount seriously affects one's health, and as a parent, it is your job to protect your child's health and welfare. You could say, "Yes, smoking is wrong, but I don't want you to make the same mistake."

29. If my daughter has been involved with drugs and her peer group consists of users too, how can I help her get new friends who are a better influence?

Forbid her from seeing her old friends. If her involvement with drugs is a problem, take her to counseling immediately. In order to help her get new friends, acknowledge how difficult it is, and offer to provide alternative activities to encourage new friendships. And then be supportive of her new friends.

30. If I confront my son with my suspicions of a drug habit, what can I do and how can I approach him?

The only way to know for sure is to take him to a doctor for a urine test.

31. How can I get my kid to go for a urine test?

Tell your kid he has no choice, and if he refuses, you will have to assume he is guilty of using drugs. Then treat the problem from that stance immediately by seeking counseling for your adolescent.

32. What if my kid responds, "You don't trust me?"

Say, "That's right—my responsibility as a parent is to keep you drug free, and my decision is in your best interest."

33. My sixteen-year-old daughter has her own job and car, and uses these as grounds for being independent, saying that she does not have to answer to us. She has been staying out later and later, sometimes until three or four A.M., and is often drunk. What can we do?

Make an appointment for her to see a counselor immediately. Take the keys away, despite the fact it is her car. This is a life-threatening situation which must be dealt with unequivocally. To be on the safe side, you might also take the car to a friend's house where she cannot find it.

34. What should I do if my teenager is arrested and jailed for possession of drugs? Should I bail him out?

Yes. Use the fact he was caught as a blessing, but get him into treatment immediately.

35. What if my teenager has been jailed repeatedly?

While you might be angry and want him to learn a lesson by staying in jail, the fact is that he needs your help and you should not give up on him. You have a legal responsibility for your child if he is under eighteen, so although he may not listen or cooperate with your attempt to get him treatment, you cannot throw him out. If your teenager is over eighteen, it may be that you need to let go if he still refuses help. However, such a decision should be made in connection with a counselor specializing in working with adolescents.

36. Is the cause for drug problems always low self-esteem, a broken home, peer pressure or confused thinking?

For 98% of the cases, this is true. If it seems that a well-adjusted kid becomes an addict, you are not looking beyond the facade; there is a deep, underlying problem. But, two things must be addressed: the drug problem, as well as the underlying one. Although some therapists just deal with the underlying problem, that is only half the issue.

37. I used drugs and smoked marijuana when I was a teenager and I hate what I was. But now I see my kid getting into the same scene. I've tried my hardest not to let the same thing happen to him. Is it too late or just bad blood? What can I do?

Drug addiction is not genetic. Immediately get him into therapy to get your kid off drugs. If you are doing anything wrong in your parenting, the therapist will be able to tell you so that you can improve. Concerning your adolescence, we all make mistakes, but don't dwell on past ones. Move forward to improve your family life now.

38. *I don't want my teenagers to drink or smoke, but our family is full of drinkers and smokers. How can I have any kind of authority over such a thing when a majority of our family does these things and still leads a normal life?*

Make it clear to your teenagers that these things are harmful nevertheless, and that it is your job as the parent to protect their health. Your rules are to stand and must be obeyed until they are twenty-one, at which time they may choose to do these things, but at the cost of being thrown out on their own.

39. *What is the most effective treatment for someone with a drug problem?*

The ideal treatment in most cases is the combination of psychotherapy and a support group such as Alcoholics Anonymous (AA) or Narcotics Anonymous (NA).

40. *If my daughter is already in psychotherapy, why should I put her in AA or NA?*

What psychotherapy does is to deal with the drug problem, but AA and NA are important because they provide a continual support system, as well as a chance to be with others experiencing similar problems. If your teen has a problem, she is an addict and can never use drugs or alcohol again. AA and NA continually reinforce this philosophy. They provide adult role models who have had abuse problems and have dealt with them successfully in their life, and now can sponsor other people.

41. *What is a sponsor?*

It is a member of AA or NA who has maintained sobriety for at least two years. A sponsor is one you can call twenty-four hours a day, whenever you feel tempted to break your sobriety, or just if you wish to talk with someone.

CHAPTER TWENTY-ONE

Unacceptable Behavior

Behavior of teenagers varies because teenagers are different from one another. Their behavior can make drastic, lightning-quick changes according to their feelings and moods, as I noted in the first chapter. However, there are some unacceptable behaviors which parents must deal with. Here are some examples.

Questions:

1. What do you do if your teenager threatens that he will kill himself every time there is an argument?

Tell him he is never to use that as a threat when he is angry. Just as hitting below the belt is dirty fighting, what he is doing is unfair, too. When he is angry, he can express his feelings, but he is not to threaten. Also, make it clear to him that if he ever feels that way, he is to come to you and tell you, so you can talk about it together.

Tell him that you do not fight unfairly with him by doing things like throwing scalding water in his face, so he is not allowed to fight unfairly with you either.

2. What can I do with my twelve-year-old who has a terrible temper and deals with her problems by hitting other kids?

Tell her that her behavior is unacceptable, and it will stop immediately. You will help her develop other solutions for her anger, but the next time she hits someone, she will be severely punished. Her behavior is out of control, and you must continue punishing her until she gets back into control.

3. What can I do with my twelve-year-old son who swears and curses all the time around me and my other female friends?

Tell him it is unacceptable behavior and that he may not swear around you. The next time he does, tell him he will be punished, and then take away a privilege. Keep escalating until he is back in control.

4. What do you do when your teenager carves crosses and skulls on his arm with a razor?

Immediately rush him to counseling. Self-mutilation is a symptom of much more serious problems. It is self-destructive, suicidal behavior.

Every kid I have seen who mutilates or cuts himself has been seriously depressed. What is happening is that he is telling you through his behavior that he needs help.

CHAPTER TWENTY-TWO

Out of Control

Because it is so hard to raise a teenager today, roughly one-third of the families we see at our Center have children or adolescents who are out of control. This chapter will help teach you methods to get your child or adolescent back into control.

In families with out-of-control adolescents, the teenagers go in and out of the house as they please without listening to parents, and refuse to do chores or to obey curfew. They go to school when and if they want, certainly not on a regular basis, take money whenever they want, and are totally defiant of all rules. If you are in that 35% of families with an out-of-control teenager, we will tell you in this chapter how to get back into control. If you have read the chapters on "Limit Setting" and "Punishment," and have used those strategies but they did not work, then I suggest reading this chapter very carefully.

Questions:

1. What do you do when your teenager just will not live by your limits and rules? For example, my son refuses to go to school —he is sixteen and stays in the house all day.

A short time ago I saw a single mother and her sixteen-year-old son who had not gone to school for eight months. His attitude was that he's bigger than she is, and she can't make him go to school because it is terrible, boring, stupid, etc.

He slept until noon, went surfing, came back to wait for his buddies to get out of school at 3:00, and then hung out with them until midnight or 1:00 A.M. before coming home. His mother could not do anything to change or alter his behavior.

When I met with him and asked why he did not want to go to school, he only said, "Well, I don't particularly like school." Then I called the mother in and suggested that she take a cold pitcher of water with her when she woke him up, and say, "If you do not get out of bed, I am going to pour this pitcher of water on you, which will only be the beginning." The kid replied, "My bedding will get all wet." I said, "Well, you have the option of getting up and going to school, or getting your bed all wet." The family came back a week later saying this strategy worked, and that the son was going to school. I got a note about five months later saying he was now going to school every day and getting a solid "B–" average.

Since I do not know the circumstances of your case, I cannot recommend a specific stategy of what to do. Other kids might have taken the pitcher and hit the mom with it.

Do whatever you must to get your adolescent back into control. Whatever force you have to use, whatever pressure you need to apply, do it for his own good.

2. My seventeen-year-old son hits me on the arm really hard, and becomes violent whenever he loses his temper. He is also out of control in a number of other ways. What can I do?

Do whatever you must to get back into control. You cannot allow your seventeen-year-old son to hit you. It is dangerous to you and it is not good for him. Tell him that if he hits you again you will call the police and have him arrested. And then follow through if he does. In the meantime, I would urge you to get counseling because of the physical danger.

3. My fifteen-year-old son is hanging around with a group of eighteen and nineteen-year-olds who are using drugs and do not go to school. They are an extremely bad influence on him, but he refuses to listen to me when I forbid him to see his friends.

You need to get back into control. Start by telling your son, "I will not allow you to be with these people, because they are too old, get into trouble, use drugs, and are not a good influence." Then monitor all his phone calls and physically stop him from leaving the house. If this does not work, go to counseling.

4. For many out-of-control situations you recommend counseling. How come?

It is dangerous for adolescents' health, safety, and welfare when they are out-of-control. If what I have suggested in this chapter does not work to get the teenager back into control, then you need to go to counseling. You have a responsibility and obligation to provide everything you can for your children's health, safety, and welfare—and being out of control involves all of these.

5. My twelve-year-old daughter enjoys arguing. I always get drawn in and lose sight of everything. We wind up screaming at each other.

Take control of the situation. There is no reason for you to listen to your daughter's arguing. When you feel you have heard enough, say, "Hey, that's it. I will not put up with this," and walk away. If she follows, tell her she cannot follow you, that she will be punished. And then follow through with it if she continues. Tell your daughter she has made her point, that you have heard it and your decision is made. The amount of time you are willing to tolerate your adolescent's arguing or hassling can depend on how you are feeling. If you have had a bad day at work, thirty seconds may be too much. If you are patient and are willing to listen for five or ten minutes, that is your decision, and that is fine. But again, you do not have to sit there and listen to all that arguing.

6. What do I do with my sixteen-year-old who will not listen to me, goes to his room, shuts his door, and locks it whenever I try to talk to him?

Tell him such behavior is no longer acceptable, and if he walks away from you again when you are talking, he will be punished. Tell him what his punishment will be, and enforce it.

7. How do I maintain control when my teenager goes to parties where there is drinking? She says she does not drink, but I am concerned.

Do not let any teen who lives in your home go to a party where there is drinking. In such an environment, even if your daughter really is not drinking, she will be subjected to peer pressure and incredible temptation. In addition, she could very easily find her friends using alcohol, and wind up going home in a car with someone driving under the influence. You have a responsibility to keep your daughter away from such influences and dangers.

8. What if my teenager says I am square and old-fashioned, and that everyone else lets their kids go to parties where there is drinking?

Tell him, "I will not allow it, period. I do not care what everyone else does. Here are the rules in our house. If everyone jumped in the ocean in the middle of winter, we would not let you."

9. What do you do with a fifteen-year-old daughter who stays away for days at a time and is totally out of control?

When an adolescent is this far out of control, it is clear she needs counseling. Take her immediately.

10. What can I do with my teenage son who is verbally abusive, only goes to school in the morning, and then cuts early every day?

Start punishing by denying privileges. If that does not work, tell him, "Look, we are the parents, we are going to be in charge here. You will not abuse us verbally by swearing and/or name-calling, and you will stay in school. We will do whatever we must to make this happen." Then, to make your point, take his door off the hinges and say, "This is for starters. If you do not obey the rules, we are going to escalate from here."

Let's say he doesn't obey your rules. Then you take everything out of his room, except his mattress and a few changes of clothes. Then say, "Look, this is just starters; we are going up from here. You are going to get back into control, and you are going to obey the rules of our house."

11. What if, when you think it is necessary to go as far as taking a door off the room, you cannot get your spouse to go along?

Go ahead and do it yourself. Tell your spouse that you would like his or her help in getting your teenager back into control, but you are going to do it with or without their help. The other option is to say, "We have a problem. Will you go to counseling with me so that we can figure out a joint strategy for getting our teenager back into control?" If the other parent refuses, just go to counseling anyway, and do the punishing yourself.

12. If I take the door off my teenager's room, where do I put it and all his things?

You lock it in a room in your house, put it in your garage under lock, or find a neighbor who has a place you could lock it away.

13. What if one of our two teenagers is unruly and borders on being out of control all the time, and he is influencing his younger brother?

It would be hard to stop the younger one from being influenced, so you need to clamp down on the one who is out of control.

14. Do many teenagers who are out of control have some kind

of chemical imbalance, or is there a biological basis for the problem?

A chemical imbalance would be extremely rare. If you have any doubt, go to your family physician and or a therapist to have it checked out. Statistically, it is also unusual for such behavior to have a biological cause. If you go to a counselor and she suspects such a thing, she would refer you to a medical doctor for testing. There are only a few, rare conditions which have a biological cause. Some unusual depressions, for example, are caused by hypoglycemia.

15. What do you do with a sophomore in high school who continually cuts school at least twice a week and says school is unimportant?

Tell him he is going to school every day, and the next time he cuts, you will take the door off his room and everything out except his mattress and a few changes of clothes. Tell him that this is only a beginning, and that if he continues, it will get far worse. You do everything you have to do in order to get your kid back into control.

16. What do I do about my daughter who is a punker, has spiked hair, wears ugly makeup, rarely goes to school, uses the "F" word all the time, uses drugs, and ignores my every word?

Take her to counseling and work out a plan to get back into control. For example, start by not letting her see her friends, and then insist she go to school. You punish, take the door off, take everything out, and keep escalating until you get back into control.

Here are some warning signs of adolescent suicide. Immediately rush your teenager to a therapist, if he/she ever displays any of the following symptoms.
- Noticeable change in eating habits.
- Withdrawal from friends and family and regular activities.
- Persistent boredom.
- A decline in the quality of schoolwork.
- Violent or rebellious behavior.
- Running away.
- Drug and alcohol abuse
- Unusual neglect of personal appearance.
- Difficulty concentrating.
- Radical personality change.
- Complaints about physical symptoms often related to

emotions, such as stomachache, headache, fatigue, etc.
A teenager planning to commit suicide may also:
- Give verbal "hints" with statements such as: "I won't be a problem for you much longer," "Nothing matters," or "It's no use."
- Put his/her affairs in order — example: give away his/her favorite possessions; clean his/her room; throw things away, etc.
- Become suddenly cheerful after a period of depression.

These warning signs are from the American Academy of Child Psychiatry and the American Psychiatric Association.

CHAPTER TWENTY-THREE

Running Away

Running away is one way teenagers deal with problems. Here are some ways you can treat this problem.

Questions:

1. What do you do with a fifteen-year-old boy who has run away, but lives around the area somewhere and still keeps in contact with you?

You immediately get counseling. A fifteen-year-old should not be on the street or living here or there. He should be living with his parents. Just imagine what could be going on if you do not know where he is.

2. How do you respond to an adolescent who runs away for twenty-four hours?

When she comes back, immediately forget your tendency to get angry and punish. Instead, sit down and find out what led her to run away. Adolescents do things for reasons. So based on the reason, you need to work things out so it won't happen again.

3. What do you do when your kid threatens to run away?

Do not allow him to threaten you. Say, "If you are unhappy, sit down and tell me. If you are angry, sit down and tell me that, too. But running away is not an acceptable way to deal with your problems."

CHAPTER TWENTY-FOUR

When to Take Your Teen to Counseling

Although the general attitude toward mental health has been improving greatly in this country in the last twenty years, still for some people there is a stigma associated with seeing a therapist. This, of course, is nonsense.

We believe that anyone, and especially one who has an adolescent, should see a therapist any time there is a serious problem, such as depression, poor performance in school, or poor social skills, to name a few. If a member of your family has a medical problem, such as a sprained ankle, the measles, or an infection, you don't hesitate to go to a doctor or other expert in the medical field. If someone in your family has a toothache, a cavity, or something wrong with chewing, you don't hesitate to go to a dentist. We believe that every teenager should see a therapist for a checkup at least once. Going to see a therapist is no different than going to the doctor or dentist.

The therapist is trained to help people. He or she helps people change the unhappy parts of their lives to make them happier. Therapists help people with problems to understand and correct them.

Don't hesitate to go to a therapist whenever you feel that there is a problem in your family that you cannot deal with, or that is causing someone serious unhappiness. Even if you think your problem or concern is silly, stupid, or dumb, don't hesitate to see a therapist. We would much rather see you go to a therapist and be told that you don't need to be there, than to let a problem become more severe, because then it is usually more difficult to deal with in therapy.

Ninety percent of the adolescents we see in therapy should have been brought in sooner than they were. Many parents make the mistake of thinking, "It's just a phase and he'll grow out of it," "He's having a bad time now, but things will get better," or, "We'll just wait a little while longer before we do something."

Many parents seem to think that if they ignore the problem it will go away. However, it seldom does. The problem usually becomes magnified. The longer you wait to bring an adolescent with a problem to a therapist, the longer it takes to correct the problem.

We can give you some guidelines to use to help you determine when to bring your teen to a therapist, but remember, these are just guidelines. When you suspect there may be a problem, don't hesitate. Make an appointment to see a therapist.

Guidelines:

1. School

When teens are doing poorly in school, particularly if the grades in elementary school and junior high were much better, and then suddenly fall off in high school, they should be seen by a therapist. When teens are being disciplined in school for poor social behavior, or when they are cutting classes or not going to school, they should be seen by a therapist.

2. Law

When teens do anything that gets themselves involved with the criminal justice system, they should be seen by a therapist. If teens are breaking the law, but haven't been caught yet, they should be seen by a therapist. Don't assume that "boys will be boys" and ignore this sign of a problem. When teens continually gets tickets with their car or have accidents, when they shoplift, burglarize homes, do vandalism, steal money from parents, or the like, they need to see a therapist.

3. Peers

When teens have friends you do not approve of, destructive youngsters who are influencing your teenagers in their destructive ways, they need to see a therapist. If all their friends are like this, the chances are they're in with a bad crowd, and there is a specific reason for this. A therapist can help find out why.

4. Drugs

Any teen who uses marijuana, amphetamines, barbiturates, PCP (angle dust), cocaine, LSD (acid), heroin, or any type of drug, should be *rushed* to a therapist. If you suspect that your youngsters are using marijuana, check out their behavior. Are they showing a lack of responsibility, are they dropping off in school, or have they changed their circle of friends? Watch for repeated usages and psychological dependency.

5. Alcohol

Watch for the misuse of alcohol, frequent use of alcohol, a lack of control of the amount of alcohol consumed, and/or irrational and irresponsible behavior when using alcohol.

6. Depression

Adolescents who mope around, feel "down" all the time, don't seem to have much energy, say all they're doing is feeling blue, don't seem to enjoy life, appear miserable all the time, and just don't seem happy, should be seen by a therapist. Teens who are lonely and withdrawn, who have difficulty making friends, who seldom go out on weekends with any friends, who seldom or never go to friends' homes, also need to be seen by a therapist.

7. Suicidal Thoughts

Immediately see a therapist if your teen makes any suicidal statements or gives any warning signs. For example, these warnings might be if your teen talks about ending their life or doing away with themself; says that they would be better off dead, that life is not worth living, that they're feeling blue, that they are totally hopeless and their life will never change so they want to go to sleep and never wake up; says they'll get even with you by killing themself, or any similar statements. A parent doesn't have the training to evaluate a suicidal statement. Go to a professional to evaluate such statements. Adolescent suicides are at their highest level ever, and the figure climbs higher each year.

8. Poor Self-Image

Although it is normal for teens to have doubts about their self-image during adolescence, an extremely poor self-image will affect how they achieve in school, how they feel about themselves, and how they do later on in life. Teens who seem not to like themselves, who seem down on themselves all the time, rarely seem to enjoy themselves, whose self-esteem and self-concept seem to be at a dangerously low ebb, should be seen by a therapist.

9. Hearing Voices or Hearing Things

This is a critical item. If teenagers should ever tell you that they think people are following them, think that they hear voices or other people talking to them, they should be seen by a therapist *immediately*.

10. Severe Weight Problems

If teens stop eating, lose weight, refuse to eat much of anything, continually tell you that they're too fat, when in reality they are not at all fat, and persist in such behavior, they should be taken to a therapist *immediately*. Also, teenagers who are overweight should be taken to a therapist.

11. Rebelliousness at Home

If teens are acting more rebellious than normal, stomping out of the house when they are angry, staying away for hours at a time, refusing to do any chores, not cooperating even minimally with the family, being totally defiant all the time, have them checked out with a therapist.

12. Sexual Activity

There are well over one million teenage pregnancies each year. If your son or daughter is having sex, it is a good idea to take the teenager to a therapist for a general mental health checkup. It is amazing that in this day so many teens don't know the first thing about birth control, venereal diseases or AIDS. What is even more amazing is that teens who do know about birth control methods don't use them. These teens get pregnant because they want to, either consciously or unconsciously. They have tremendously low self-esteem. For this kind of teenage girl, getting pregnant affirms her femininity, makes her feel like a real woman, and compensates for her very low self-esteem. In addition, many girls consciously or unconsciously want to get pregnant because they want the status of being a mother, and immaturely feel that they are capable of it. For a teenage boy with low self-esteem, impregnating a girl means that he's a man, and affirms his masculinity by showing he can get his girl pregnant. This compensates for his feelings of low self-esteem.

13. Problems Between Spouses

Often one parent takes a position that the other parent feels is totally unreasonable, and that parent won't budge. Part of the function of therapy is to help educate parents not only about what is age-appropriate behavior for teens, but what is appropriate behavior for parents.

14. Loners

Teens who are withdrawn, have few or no friends, who spend

large amounts of time alone, should be seen by a therapist.

15. Problems Between Family Members

If youngsters refuse to problem-solve or to enter into a contract, or families are not able to resolve problems using these methods, they should see a therapist.

These are some of the major reasons and criteria parents should use in deciding when to go to a therapist. However, they are by no means all-inclusive. You should remember that the time to go to the therapist is when you suspect there is a problem that isn't being handled well by one or more members of your family. You need to remember, too, that what you're doing is simply consulting an expert about a problem.

Questions:

1. My 17-year-old son comes home drunk often. He is rapidly going downhill in school, going from "A's" to "D's" and "F's" now. When he comes home, he yells at me. Does he need counseling?

Absolutely. We are seeing a pattern of difficulties in a number of areas: school, an explosive, angry behavior, and alcohol abuse.

2. How do you get help for a teenager who doesn't live in your home and really needs help? She is nineteen, living with her boyfriend, is depressed, and takes pills all the time.

There are a couple of things you could do. First, go to her and say, "I am really concerned about your behavior." Tell her what your concerns are, and that you would like to take her to a counselor. If she refuses, then say something to the effect that she should just try it five times, that it is only one hour a week for five weeks. She would have nothing to lose. If she still refuses, say, "Look, I love you; I am concerned about you. If you ever want to go to a counselor, let me know and I will help you find one and get you there."

3. What can I do if my fifteen-year-old son is not willing to go to a counselor?

The first thing is to explain what counseling is all about. You might say that if anyone in our family had a bad toothache, they would go to the dentist, and if anyone in our family had a really bad sore throat, they would go to the doctor. So if anyone in our family has something they are unhappy about, they are going for counseling.

The second thing is to say, "Look, just try it once a week for eight weeks. If you don't like it you don't have to go back." Another approach is to say, "You don't have any choice. Get in the car." Then you make it happen.

One of the things we do at our Center if these methods do not work, is to go out and meet the kid at your home, at school, or at a neutral place like the bowling alley or McDonald's.

4. Does counseling ever include anti-depressants?

Our philosophy of doing counseling and therapy usually does not include drugs or medication. In a rare case (one in a hundred), we might recommend a medical consultation for an anti-depressant or another type of drug. There are other extremely unusual circumstances when we would recommend a drug, but generally we are against drugs.

Drugs that we are not real happy about, but seem effective, are drugs like Ritalin for hyperactive kids. Often what we will do when a youngster who is on Ritalin comes into our Center, is that we will "base line him," in cooperation with his medical doctor. This means we take the kid off Ritalin to see how he gets along without it. Most often he can't, since he's been on it a certain amount of time. It seems that this is a drug which is a necessary evil for this problem.

5. What if my teenager lies to me and her friends, fabricating her stories to the point of getting in trouble?

Such behavior says to me how unhappy such an adolescent must be, and what poor self-esteem she must have to lie so much. It may be that at this point she doesn't know the difference between a lie and the truth. Getting in trouble for such behavior emphasizes how serious the situation is; and in this case, counseling would be very beneficial.

6. What if you have been to a counselor and it did not work?

We get that question often, and we suggest you look on Page 134 of *How To Live With Your Teenager: A Survivor's Handbook For Parents* for help in choosing a counselor. It is important to choose a counselor who works well with teenagers and specializes in adolescent psychotherapy. It is also important, as suggested in the above-mentioned section, to choose a counselor who knows how to engage kids well, and can get them to talk and be part of the therapy. So choose a counselor carefully, and try it again.

7. Our teenage son gets into trouble a lot and we are continu-

ally restricting him. But he will climb out a window and not stay home.

Your son is out of control and you should go to counseling immediately.

8. What kind of therapy is available for my seventeen-year-old son who is using marijuana and cocaine? Would group therapy help him?

I can tell you how the procedures at our Center work. What we do is to see the parent the first time to get information and a case history. The second time we see the adolescent, and the third time we meet with the parents again to give our recommendation. Primarily, we have three ways of treating adolescents: individual therapy, family therapy, and group therapy. Because each teen has a different problem, we would base the treatment on what would be best for him or her. One of the three methods above, or a combination, might be best. Group therapy is particularly good for a number of different types of adolescents. For example, an extremely shy, isolated kid who does not have any friends could use group therapy to learn the specific skills necessary to build relationships. Sometimes this kind of therapy can be very effective with kids who have drug problems, because they listen to their peers better than to adults. But again, until we do a thorough case history, we cannot make a recommendation as to what would be best.

9. How do you get a father of a teenager to go to counseling when all the family members should be involved in the therapy process?

Simply tell him it is very important that he participate in his child's treatment because he is a member of the family, and it will help his teenager get better, sooner. If this does not work, when you get to counseling you can discuss with the counselor ways to involve the adolescent's father.

10. What do you do with a teenager who is a chronic runaway? He stays away for three to four days at a time and sometimes longer. He isn't going to school and is using drugs.

It is clear that just about every area of his life is dysfunctional, so you need to take him to counseling immediately, and get back in control for his own benefit.

11. Do you go to a counselor if you are not sure? How do you ever know?

We have the conviction that if one goes to a physician or a dentist once a year for a checkup, one should consider going to a counselor once a year for a checkup. Going to a counselor once to get a professional outsider's evaluation certainly will not hurt. Most families we see would have been better off if they had come earlier.

12. How long does counseling take?

Unlike many things in medicine, where a doctor can predict the length of time needed to get better, the amount of counseling a person may need is almost impossible to predict. Your question would be answered differently by each of the varying styles of therapy and the many approaches to counseling.

The therapy at our Center is, by practice, short-term counseling. Everything which causes a person to be the way he or she is goes back to childhood. However, we do not believe we need to go back that far to help a person with his problems. Since so many of the adolescents who come to us have severe problems, we want to use methods which will help them as quickly as possible. Otherwise, they would continue to deteriorate in the process of prolonged counseling.

You may want to ask the therapist you choose whether he or she uses short or long-term methods. Also, see if the counselor uses family therapy, since it really offers the advantage of making therapy go much quicker and is very effective.

13. My fifteen-year-old has been in therapy for four months now, going every week by himself. He has always been a great con-artist and manipulator, and we really believe he is conning the counselor.

This is one of the reasons we believe so strongly in family therapy. When the family is involved, they can report to the counselor every week as to how well the adolescent is doing. We use family therapy in just about every case where an adolescent is involved.

14. When wouldn't you use family therapy?

We would not use it if older teenagers of seventeen, eighteen, or nineteen told us they are willing to come in for therapy only on the condition that their parents not be involved. If, in fact, we see them as mature and adult-like, we will respect their maturity, and the fact that they are pulling away from the family. However, family therapy is the basis of our counseling.

15. My fourteen-year-old daughter has run away and is living

with a nineteen-year-old who has introduced her to alcohol and drugs. What would make a fourteen-year-old want to associate with a nineteen-year-old and stay involved with alcohol and drugs? What do I do?

We cannot answer your question without getting a lot more background from you. What I can tell you is that your teen is out of control and you should not tolerate it. I would go get her and make her stay at home. It is completely inappropriate for a fourteen-year-old to live with a nineteen-year-old. Also I would immediately get counseling for her.

16. *Last year my son was getting "B's" and "A's." This year he is getting "F's." I help him every evening with his homework for two hours, but he will not turn it in. What can I do?*

This is a situation for which I would recommend counseling. Obviously his behavior is self-defeating, and if it has been happening for so long, with such severe deterioration, it is apparent counseling is needed.

17. *What do you do with a thirteen-year-old who runs away to live with her grandmother? She is out of control both at home and at her grandmother's, and her grandmother doesn't even want her there.*

You get her and say, "Look, there is a problem in the family. You are unhappy and we are unhappy, so we will all go to family counseling."

18. *My ten-year-old is having a lot of headaches and stomachaches. Recently I learned that one year ago, when he was at his father's (we are divorced), he drove a tractor and ran over a five-year-old boy. His father put pressure on him not to say anything because he knew I would forbid him to go back to his father's. Should I take him to a counselor?*

Absolutely. It is possible he is having many guilt feelings about running over the other boy, and it is not too late to go to counseling so he can talk about his feelings. You also need to deal with his father concerning his responsibility for his son's mental and physical well-being.

19. *What do you do if there is a divorce, and the father of the adolescent is the problem and will not be involved in the therapy?*

Go to therapy anyway, tell the therapist the problem, and seek his help in getting the father involved in therapy.

20. What can be done about an eleven-year-old who always beats kids up? He is always getting suspended from school for fighting, and the next time he will be expelled.

It is almost always a sign of poor self-esteem, unhappiness, and uncontrolled anger. Since it is a destructive pattern of behavior which does not appear to be stopping, I would suggest counseling.

21. Is individual counseling better or is Alateen?

Depending on the needs of the adolescent, which can be determined in the first few visits, either one could be acceptable. Alateen, the support group for children of alcoholic parents, often can be used in conjunction with counseling.

22. What do you do when your fourteen-year-old daughter is sexually active and is not involved with a particular boyfriend?

To me this indicates a number of problems. She has extremely poor self-esteem, and may feel that being sexually active will make her more popular. Teenagers with such low self-esteem become convinced that the only way they will be accepted is by having sex. This situation requires counseling urgently.

23. My teenager refuses to go to counseling because he does not want to talk about his problems outside the family.

If he needs counseling, I would take him no matter what he says. An adolescent who is apparently unhappy does not have the maturity to determine whether he needs counseling or not. If he had broken his leg in three places in a car accident, you would not let him make the choice of whether or not to go to a doctor. Do not let him make the choice—going cannot be harmful.

24. I just learned my fifteen-year-old daughter has been sexually active for two years with a large number of boys. She knows I cannot stand looking at her and have lost all respect for her.

I would suggest that you start by going to counseling yourself until you can understand your feelings of disappointment and anger toward your daughter. Then work on the problem of your daughter's low self-esteem, and also work as a family to make the unhappy parts of your family life happier.

25. My thirteen-and-a-half-year-old daughter, whose grades are going down in school, took our pickup last Saturday and was driving around quite drunk with a bunch of other kids.

She has become very moody, and sits and stares at a poster in her room for hours. Do you think that this will pass?

What I do all day is listen to teenagers talk about their problems and their lives. Very often they tell me they are confused. Most of the time, they really are. A lot of changes occur in kids' lives at this age. Usually around the sixth, seventh, or eighth grade they move from grammar school with one teacher to junior high school with five or six. A few years later they move to high school with even more teachers and more students. Most kids go through puberty around this age; the hormones surge through their bodies and they begin experiencing and feeling things they have never felt before. Often they do not know what is going on, and they lack the skills to verbalize it.

Kids signal us with their behavior. Behavior such as drastic, sullen moods over long periods of time, deteriorating performance in school, problems with alcohol, a life-threatening situation, stealing the parents' car and driving around drunk for hours, tells us something. This youngster is giving us a loud and clear message that says, "Hey, I am hurting; I need help." Because kids often cannot signal us with words, they signal us with their behavior. Your daughter's behavior is a scream and a cry for help, and a signal that something is going on in her life that is causing her to threaten her life. She certainly needs immediate counseling before she hurts herself and others.

26. *My kids have been in counseling for seven months and the therapist refuses to tell me anything. My own daughter does not seem to be getting any better. Whenever I talk to the therapist, she says she cannot violate the childrens' confidentiality. Otherwise, they would not trust her. What can I do?*

Without knowing all the details of the case, we would still consider treating this as we do most other cases: through family therapy. This is the quickest way we know to help kids and families, and also gives the parent a clear idea of what is going on.

You also have the option of switching therapists if you feel you are not seeing any results after seven months.

27. *I am from the old school where no one ever went to counseling; we solved our problems on our own. Isn't counseling just a crutch? And what happened to the old spirit of hard work, buckle down, and your problems will take care of themselves?*

Your question raises a number of issues. One is what the fundamental purpose of counseling is supposed to be. It is simply to take the unhappy parts of peoples lives and make them happier. Twenty years ago there was a stigma attached to going to counseling. Most people believed that if you went to counseling you were nuts, crazy, or psycho. Unfortunately, there is still a stigma with some people about going to counseling.

One of the major changes about psychotherapy is the public's attitude and awareness about it. In terms of counseling, the only major difference between adolescents being treated and those who are not, is that the parents of those in counseling had enough sense to bring them in to get help for their problems. It is not that their problems are particularly greater than kids who do not get counseling, but that the parents realized that there would be more immediate benefits for their children and family. Again, people who would not hesitate to take their kids to the dentist for toothaches or cavities should not hesitate to take their kids to a counselor to solve unhappy parts of their lives.

The other major issue your question raises is that twenty years ago raising a teenager was much easier. It has never been harder than now to raise a teenager. We need to open ourselves to all the options available to help our kids overcome their problems and grow up as healthy as possible.

Some problems cannot be worked out just by force of discipline and hard work. Sometimes kids become physiologically addicted to drugs or alcohol. Sometimes they cannot change no matter how much willpower they have. It would be the same as if I asked you to flap your arms and fly; you could not do it. Many times kids cannot change by using only force of will, since the patterns they have established and the events which have led them to establish these patterns do not let them do otherwise. Many problems are impossible to change by force of will, but can be changed by competent counseling.

28. I suspect my kid is using drugs, but I want to find out for sure. How can I?

Arrange with your doctor or a medical laboratory to take your son in on a Monday and get his urine checked. That way you will know for sure. If there are drugs in the urine, then you need to go to counseling.

29. If I did that with my fifteen-year-old and there were no drugs in the urine, he would say I didn't trust him, and I had betrayed him, and we would never communicate again.

Tell him you have a responsibility as a parent to ensure his health, safety, and welfare, and you are sorry he feels that way, but you are going to test him on a regular basis if you have any suspicion. That is your responsibility as a parent, and if he is clean, there will be no problem.

30. My kid has spiked hair with colors, wears black all the time, hangs around other kids who are dressed in black, and won't stop using the "F" word. Should I bring him in to counseling?

Most kids who are into punk and heavy metal music use drugs. One thing you might consider doing is get a urine check. What seems to happen is that these kids follow a typical pattern, where they become more and more involved with drugs, and become more and more alienated as the problems increase. This is a situation which calls for counseling, not necessarily because of the rebellious appearance of your son, but because of the endangering atmosphere of his subculture.

> THEME FOUR:
> Special Family Issues Involving Teenagers

CHAPTER TWENTY-FIVE

Parenting

Parenting in the 1980's and '90's is more difficult and complicated than ever before. It is at once discouraging as well as rewarding. Here are some ways to do the work of parenting.

Questions:

1. *How do you handle parenting when two people see parenting in a different light and have different views on everything?*

That is an often-asked question. First of all, people generally see issues in many different ways, including parenting. Two people will have different ideas or opinions about a TV show, the color of the carpet, whether they like Chinese or Italian food, or what movie to see.

It is so complicated raising a teenager that I am not surprised people have different views. When parents disagree, I suggest that they go behind locked doors and compromise. It is crucial to present a united front to adolescents. Otherwise, they will play one parent off against the other and manipulate both of you.

2. *What do you do when one parent is strict and the other is not?*

Go behind closed doors and reach a compromise. Then you can present a united front to your teenagers so they won't manipulate one parent against the other.

3. *Is there any reward in parenting? All I ever feel is anger or frustration.*

The research indicates that 75% to 80% of parents would not have had children if they could make the choice today. The research is also clear that the happiest times for parents were before they had kids. Parents seem to dislike being a parent. Especially when they are a parent of a teenager. Frequently teens are loud, obnoxious, unappreciative and selfish, and they give parents a very difficult time. The good news is that once they are gone and grown, and you have done a good job parenting, you can have a satisfying, close relationship with them and enjoy them much more.

4. What do I do if my wife doesn't discipline and finds it hard to do?

Make her aware how important it is, and get counseling for her if she is unable to do it. The chances are that in your family your teenagers have gotten away with a lot which is not good for them. What happens is that you become the enemy and the "bad guy," which is not fair to you, while your wife becomes the "good guy."

5. I am really good friends with my daughter and find it hard to discipline her. What do you suggest?

The most important thing an adolescent needs is a parent. A parent has to set limits, stick to the limits, enforce them, and discipline. It is important for the parent to develop a relationship where the adolescent feels comfortable talking to the parent. But it is inappropriate and wrong for the parent to become her friend. The teenager needs to pull away from the parent, and cannot do that as easily if the parent is a friend. Also, if you are a friend, you cannot be the strict adult disciplinarian and role model. I would suggest that you work hard on disciplining and setting limits. It does not mean you cannot be friendly towards your daughter, but it is wrong and inappropriate for you to be her friend when she needs your guidance the most.

CHAPTER TWENTY-SIX

Divorce

As a result of the enormous amount of divorces today, adolescents often find themselves in very difficult situations.

Questions:

1. What do you do in a divorced family where the teenager will play one parent against the other?

Hopefully, you can talk to your "ex" and communicate well. If you cannot, which happens quite frequently, you might try explaining the situation to the adolescent. For example, your teens will come home from their father's and say to you, "It is more fun at Dad's. He lets us stay up until midnight and you make us go to bed at l0:00 o'clock." You might try the following approach: "Look, when you go to two friends' houses, like Joey and Billy, they have different rules. For example, Joey's family may not have the TV on at dinner because they want time just for their family to talk and relax, and they feel the TV interrupts them. Bill's family, on the other hand, may want the TV on because they find it relaxing, and the background from the TV to be soothing. They like listening and watching the TV as they eat. Your dad and I have different rules in our house, just as Billy's and Joey's parents have different rules in theirs. I can appreciate the fact that it is hard for you to adjust from one set of rules to the other, but it will be OK. Now you can understand why different people have different sets of rules, since no two people are alike."

Unfortunately, many divorces do not end amicably, and many parents have a tendency to put the other parent down and call them names on a regular basis.

What is imperative to remember is that when you put the parent down, you put the teenager down, since each kid is a part of both parents. Our rule is to never put a parent down.

So, rather than saying, "Your dad's rules are terrible, and I don't agree with him. He is a bad parent for letting you stay up until midnight," it is much better to say as we indicated, "Hey, there are different rules for different families."

2. If the teen threatens to pack her bags and go live with the father when she is angry, do you let her go?

No. Say to your teen, "That is an unacceptable way to handle your anger. If you want to talk about living with your father, that is fine; come and talk to me. If you really want to do that we will discuss it, but it is not acceptable to use that as an escape when you are angry. Instead, you should tell me what you are angry about, and we will talk about it."

3. What do you do in a divorce when your "ex" won't become involved with therapy, and he is part of the problem?

There is nothing you can do if he refuses to come to therapy. Be sure to take your teen to therapy and brainstorm with the therapist to see if you can get the father involved. Always leave the door open for the father to be involved. It may not happen at the beginning, but with luck, he'll become involved somewhat later in the therapy.

4. What do you do when your teenager lives with his father, and his father lets him drink, stay out late at night, and break rules, including not going to school?

Once a kid becomes non-custodial (i.e., when he doesn't live in your house) in reality you lose a great deal of influence. The first thing I would suggest is to talk with your "ex" about the type of situation in which your son is living. If that does not get any results and you have evaluated the situation carefully, you should realize that you are not going to be very effective trying to enforce rules when he lives in another house. What I would suggest is to act as a caring, friendly, supportive parent, and try to build and enhance your relationship and rapport. There is really not much you can do to enforce rules, because (a) the teen is not in your house, and (b) the husband won't cooperate. But also remember that if you keep nagging and complaining to your adolescent, more than likely he will stop listening to you altogether, and there won't be an effective stratagy in building your relationship. Nor will you get him to change his behavior to obey the rules you think are important.

CHAPTER TWENTY-SEVEN

Stepparenting

There are 25 million families in the United States where there are stepchildren and stepparents. Fifty percent of these families end in divorce. As hard as it is to be a parent, being a stepparent is even harder. This chapter begins to help you with some issues in stepparenting adolescents.

Stepparenting with adolescent children (I consider adolescent children as ages 10 and above) is extremely difficult. It is tough for the teenager, the stepparent, and for the biological parent. Part of the problem is that people often have unrealistic expectations. Many times the stepparent is the father who moves in with a mother and her biological children. Usually the stepfather cares about the kids, otherwise he would not have gotten involved and married a women with adolescent children. His expectation is often, "I will be especially nice to these kids, support them, give them some discipline, and in three or four months we will all be a happy family." The perspective the adolescent has is, "Why should I take orders from this new guy?" Immediately it becomes very complicated and can quickly deteriorate. For example, the adolescent can come into the living room and turn his TV program on, but now that his stepdad is there, the stepdad can often insist on watching his own program. The adolescent feels resentful that there is an adult he does not know who is automatically giving him orders.

After a while the relationship often degenerates, until (anywhere from two to four months later) the stepparent and adolescent hate each other, and the biological mother feels torn between the two. What works best in this situation is that the biological parent should do all the disciplining and the stepparent should act as a healthy, constructive adult role model for the stepchild. Again, this is very much against what most stepparents want to do. They want to go in and help the stepmom reestablish discipline and bring order to an often chaotic house. What we know from long experience is that it does not work. The adolescent's perception is that they are giving up a great deal when the stepfather or mother comes into their lives. Because of their age, they will be rebelling, and it is convenient to direct the rebellion against the stepparent who does not have a bond with them.

Another common expectation is that the stepparent and adolescent will like each other. This is difficult. If the average adult met one hundred teenagers on the street socially, how many of them would they really like? Our guess is very few, simply because most of the time many adolescents are difficult to like. Usually it takes a long time for the adolescent and the stepparent to get to know each other, let alone get to like each other. Furthermore, there is a psychological developmental obstacle to the process of the stepparent bonding with an adolescent. It is age-appropriate for the adolescent to rebel, not to want to spend time with the parent or stepparent, not to want to talk to the parent or stepparent, and to become less open, more secretive, and move away from the family. If the stepparent tries to pursue his relationship actively, most of the time it will backfire. He will just keep chasing and the adolescent will continue running away, maybe even faster.

Again, it is best for the stepparent to take the role of the constructive adult role model, while the biological parent does all the discipline. This does not mean that if the stepparent walks in the door and the TV is too loud he cannot ask his stepson to turn it down. What it does mean is that the terms of setting limits and forcing punishment should be left up to the the biological parent. This is also true if the stepparent is a woman living with the man's biological children.

There is a bonding process which takes place with biological children and parents. It begins in infancy and develops over time. It simply happens between parents and children as they grow and become adults.

When I ask stepparents how long they think it takes to establish a bond with their stepchild, the usual answer is somewhere between four and six months, and sometimes even two or three months. If a bond is established between a stepparent and adolescent, the research clearly shows it takes between four and seven years. Again, this is because of the nature of the rebellion process in adolescents. Frequently it never occurs, and that is OK, too. It is hoped that the teenager and stepparent living together will treat each other politely and have respect for each other. There is no rule that a bond or relationship has to develop. Remember, these suggestions apply only if the child is ten or above when the stepparent moves into the family.

Questions:

1. Why isn't my moving into my stepson's and stepdaughter's life a great thing for them? Their mother does not have to work, she switched from a full-time job to a part-time job, and I can afford things that they need, such as braces, gymnastic lessons and clothes. Why do they hate me so much?

From an adolescent's point of view, which is usually selfish, the negatives outweigh the positives when a stepparent moves in. The negatives can be: 1. This person takes time away from me and my mom. 2. Before, I could get away with murder with my mom; now she has support in forcing discipline. 3. My mom wasn't around much when she worked late in the evenings. Now she doesn't have to work so much, so I can't pull all the stuff I used to. 4. I used to be able to play the music as loud as I wanted in my house, and now my stepdad won't let me. 5. I used to be able to watch any TV program I wanted to; now I can't because my stepdad watches what he wants most of the time. 6. I have to watch myself all the time and not make too much noise; otherwise my stepdad yells and gets angry. 7. My stepdad's children come in every other weekend and I have to share my room with brats who continally go through my drawers and mess up all my stuff. I hate them. 8. My stepdad favors his own children and yells at us. 9. My mom used to make whatever I wanted for dinner; now most of the time she makes what my stepdad likes. I don't get what I want as much as I did before. 10. My stepdad doesn't like my favorite clothes and buys me all this square stuff. 11. I had to give up all my friends, my neighborhood, and my youth group, and move into my stepdad's house where it's all his things and none of ours. It is clear that from the adolescent's point of view, mom or dad getting married to a stepparent can be strongly negative.

2. I am really disappointed. I've just been married for eight months, and no matter what I do, including taking my stepchildren to different places, buying things for them and spending a lot of time with them, they don't care or appreciate it, and they never say thank you.

It is certainly easy to understand your unhappiness and frustration. As I mentioned earlier in the book, one of the age-appropriate behaviors of adolescents is selfishness, where teenagers are often completely and totally selfish. They do not often, if ever, appreciate what biological parents or other adults in their life do, so it would not necessarily change for a stepparent. Your expectation of getting thanks or appreciation is understandable, yet I do not think it is very realistic. One of the characteristics of a relationship between a teenager and parent or stepparent is that the teenager is 99% taking while the parent is 99% giving. I would encourage you to keep giving, and again, to consider changing your expectation about getting much, if anything, back.

You must keep in mind, though, why you should continue giving, and not lose heart. The answer is seen in the difference between a war and a battle. In order to win the war between you and your teenager, you will have to put up with his rebellion now. The battle is what goes on everyday, the fighting and bickering, and it is not as important to win this everyday battle. What is more important is to win the war. What will your relationship be like with your teen when he or she is twenty-five? To win the war is to eventually have a meaningful, close and personal relationship with your child after the rebellions have ceased.

3. A friend of mine and her adopted stepdaughter have never gotten along. They fought for the first few months and the girl ran away repeatedly. Why was that?

Without more information, I can only guess. When there are conflicts between a parent and a biological child, there is a long history since infancy of bonding and caring, and the establishing of a relationship. Despite the fact adolescents are often full of turmoil, there is caring and love beneath the adolescent's harsh words and actions. With a newly-adopted child, there is no history of bonding or ties to fall back on. The teen's typical attitude might be, "Hey, this is a lady I've lived with for a couple of months, and I cannot stand her so I'll just leave."

4. You say that I should stay out of disciplining. What do I do when my fifteen-year-old stepdaughter argues and yells rudely at her mother?

What many stepparents do is rush in and support the biological parent. Frequently, while it is successful for biological parents, it does not work very well with stepparents. What I suggest is to let the two of them battle it out, and if you cannot stand being around it, ask them to leave the room, or you leave the room and give your wife support later. Again, because there has not been a bonding process, it usually does not work out well when the stepparent actively does the disciplining with the child. It often causes more resentment in the stepchild than it gains. It may bring an immediate result because the stepchild has some fear, but in the long run it develops animosity, which is taken out against both the stepparent and the biological parent.

5. What about the stepparents who have been with the child since they have been four or five?

What I said previously does not apply then, since there is almost always a bonding process. The stepparent should treat the child as if he were a biological child. The other important difference of why the bonding process is easier if the stepparent moves in when the child is one to nine years old is that the child is not in a state of rebellion.

6. What about a stepfamily where the biological mother has out-of-control teenagers, and refuses to discipline them because she just does not know how? As a stepparent, if I come in and discipline them, then will I get a lot of trouble?

Basically, the biological parent should be the major disciplinary factor in all important issues, such as curfew, violation of rules, grades, health and safety, etc. If the biological parent can't or won't do that, then you may have to step in on a temporary basis. Be prepared that the stepchildren will hate you, although that may be the lesser of the two issues. This is a situation where counseling would be beneficial, and where the biological mother could learn to become an effective parent.

7. What do I do if I have three teenage stepchildren, their father is traveling frequently, and I am the only one at home to discipline them?

One method of working with this situation is to sit down in a family meeting and have the father say, "These are the rules of the house. Because I am gone a lot, I have asked your stepmom to be in charge. At my request, she will be disciplining you and having you obey the rules. She is going to act as my substitute." This way is best because the biological father is giving his permission for the stepmother to do the disciplining. However, if the punishments can wait until the biological father comes home, then the family would be better off.

8. What can I do when my stepchild is deliberately trying to drive me crazy, especially when his biological mother is not around?

All adolescents, including stepchildren, will continually test parents to see what they can get away with. This is part of the age-appropriate behavior of adolescents. If this is occurring, you need to set limits and enforce them. You have to be the one who is the boss, and you cannot allow the adolescent to belittle you, push you around, or harass you.

CHAPTER TWENTY-EIGHT

Single Parents

Difficult as it can be to raise a teenager with two parents, the single parent almost always has even more problems. A single parent is usually a mother, but gradually more fathers are joining the ranks of the single parent.

A typical day in the life of a single parent starts out early in the morning when she gets up, gets dressed, cooks breakfast, makes sure the children have something to eat, gets them out to the bus or the carpool with books and lunch snacks in tow. Next, she puts the milk and butter back into the refrigerator and stacks the breakfast dishes—there is rarely time to wash them or to make beds or to pick up the living room. She rushes to her car or to the corner to catch the bus, hoping that traffic is light so she can arrive at work on time.

She works hard all day, she may even have had an urgent call from school which she handled as well as she could on the phone, but probably worried about it all afternoon. Now at last, the work day is over and she can start for home. Out she goes to face the rush hour traffic, first stopping at the market to pick up an item or two missed during her weekly shopping. And finally, she's home. Home to a house that still has the breakfast dishes in the sink, beds unmade, and a messy living room. Where to start first?

But, before she can do anything, she remembers the phone call from school. First things first, she tackles the school problem with her teen. When that's taken care of, one of the other children needs her.

It's 7 p.m. now and she's just starting supper. One of the teens has the stereo on as high as it will go. The youngest child is yelling at him to lower it so she can hear her favorite television program. She finally gets dinner on the table, and if she's lucky, has the kitchen clean and the living room picked up by 9 P.M. The kids had homework, so she got no help from them. The beds? Why make them? It's time to go to bed again.

When the house finally quiets down, Mom realizes that she didn't get the rent check in the mail. She meant to ask Jimmy to mail the check after dinner, and then forgot. The garbage didn't get out tonight, either. Jimmy was supposed to do it, but hasn't been keeping up with his chores lately. She must remember to talk to him about that tomorrow. Now that she finally has a chance to sit down, all she can think of is, "When will this all end? When will there be time for me? Will there ever be time enough for the kids? Is my life over?"

Soon, after everyone is in bed, she collapses into bed herself. This day is repeated five times a week. And now the weekend is here. She can barely struggle through the chores of cleaning, washing, shopping, ad infinitum. She has no spouse to turn to for support and comfort, no one to complain to, no one with whom to share the load, no one with whom to discuss things, no one with whom to laugh, no one with whom to plan for the future.

This goes on seven days a week, year after year. Add to their frustration and fatigue the fact that most single parents also have financial problems, and it's no wonder they sometimes ask themselves: "Where does it all end?"

Being a single parent is simply an incredibly difficult job, and it is almost a miracle that single parents are able to make it at all.

All of the feelings that two-parent families have toward their teenagers are usually experienced in a much deeper way by the single parent. The load is greater for the single parent. In addition to the frustration, the anger, and the rage that a single parent feels, she typically has other feelings, such as: "I would really like to get rid of this kid," "I wish I never had any children," "I wish they would go to live with their father (or mother) and never come back," "I feel like giving up," "It isn't fair." When two-parent families have these feelings, and they do, they have each other to talk things out with, they have each other for support, they can laugh about it together, and they can plan for the future together.

When the single parent has these feelings—and if she doesn't, something's wrong—she's alone; she may find it difficult to discuss these feelings with a friend or another family member.

Very often single parents will feel guilty because they think they're not doing enough for their kids, or that they're not doing things well enough. Guilt piles up on guilt, and underneath that guilt hides anger.

Acknowledge your right to feel these feelings and your anger. You're right. Life isn't fair. Your mental health will improve greatly if you can acknowledge the injustice and the unfairness in your life.

Another problem a single parent encounters is the lack of a support system. The single-parent needs to know that she's not the only person to experience this lack of support. Try to find people and groups with whom to share similar experiences. Your church or synagogue may have a single-parent group, or your community may sponsor such a group.

We believe that for your kids to be happy, you have to be happy. Try to take some time for yourself each week. Try to find people who share some of the same experiences you do. Try to become each other's support system. The better you feel about yourself, the better parent you can be to your children. They, in turn, become easier to live with because they start to feel better about themselves.

Questions:

1. I am a single parent and often feel guilty because I wish my teenager would run away. I just do not know what to do.

As I've discussed before, it is incredibly difficult being a single parent. Almost all parents, including single parents if they are really honest about their feelings under stress, have often had the following type of thoughts: "I wish my teenager were never born; I'd like to run away; I wish my teen would run away; I hate him; I wish I could strangle him; I really wish my kid were dead; I really wish I never had that kid." (In my book, *How to Live With Your Teenager: A Survivor's Handbook For Parents,* there is an entire chapter on single parenting which I highly recommend to all single parents.) There is nothing wrong with having these thoughts and feelings. Obviously, acting on them is inappropriate. It is just a signal to us, as parents, how difficult it is raising adolescents today. So your thoughts and feelings are OK and appropriate.

How one can deal with these feelings is to have a good support group. Yet I often find that single parents, as well as other parents, have no support system. What I mean by support system is someone you can call and talk to, whether it is a friend, relative or neighbor, and say something to this effect: "I have had a really bad day and want to kill my kid. He is driving me nuts. I just need to talk to someone." A support system is someone who will listen to you and be there for you.

Many single parents are understandably overwhelmed just by working and taking care of their children, so it is very important to develop a support system, and perhaps become a support for someone else in turn. Another thing I highly recommend is getting out one evening a week, even if it takes hiring a sitter, just to go window shopping, to a movie, bowling, or have a cup of coffee with a friend.

CHAPTER TWENTY-NINE

Eighteen On Up

Questions:

1. My eighteen-year-old daughter has finished high school and is working. She is going on nineteen now. Should I set a curfew for her?

Definitely. As long as she lives under your roof, you are entitled to set rules. If she does not like it, she can leave.

2. What are proper limits to set for a daughter of eighteen?

First, she must be doing something constructive, such as going to school, going to a trade school, taking classes, or working. Second, she has to do chores, since she is part of the family. Third, set limits you feel comfortable with, based on how much you trust your daughter. For example, if you do not want smoking in the house, she cannot smoke there. If you want the living room picked up at the end of the day, make that part of the agreement about living there.

3. My eighteen-year-old is threatening to leave home unless I give him permission to stay out to all hours of the night. I do not want him to leave, but I do not want him to stay out all night. What do I do?

As long as he knows that you do not want him to leave, he has a hold on you. I suggest that you make your mind up, and stick to certain standards which he must live up to or leave.

4. My nineteen-year-old lays around the house all day. She does not go to work or to school. While I agree with you about kicking her out, I am sure she will starve because she could not survive on her own.

I suggest that you tell her she needs to get into counseling. She needs to go to a counselor who can help her take the unhappy parts of her life and make them happier. When she starts going to the counselor, give her however much time you feel comfortable with for her to start school, get a job or do something else constructive. If she does not, she has to leave. You are certainly not helping her by keeping her there. Just think, she could be there till she is twenty-five, thirty, or thirty-five. I would throw her out and tell her, "Hey, we tried to help, but it is your problem, not ours."

Are You Looking For More Answers?

The Center for Family Life Enrichment, Inc. also makes available copies of Mr. Buntman's first book, *How To Live With Your Teenager: A Survivor's Handbook for Parents*. To order a copy or to order an additional copy of this book — please copy the order form below:

Mail To: Publications Division
Center for Family Life Enrichment, Inc.
3611 Farquhar Avenue Suite 3
Los Alamitos, CA 90720

For faster service on Master Card and Visa orders you may call (310) 596-8712, Pacific Time.

FREE tape cassette of Mr. Buntman's lecture "How To Live With Your Teenager" with any order

Dear Sirs:

Please ship me

___ copies of Mr. Buntman's first book *How To Live With Your Teenager: A Survivor's Handbook for Parents* at $9.95 each.

___ additional copies of this book, *How to Live with Your Teenager II: A Question and Answer Guide for Parents* at $9.95 each.

___ Free tape cassette with order (per above)

___ Total books ordered x $9.95 = $ _____

___ Please add $2.00 shipping and handling charge for the first book and $1.00 for each additional book.

Shipping $ _____

CA residents please $ _____
add 8.25% sales tax

Total amount enclosed $ _____

☐ I have enclosed my check for the amount shown above.
☐ Please bill my ☐ Master Card ☐ Visa

Credit Card Number:_____ Expiration:_____

Please ship this order to:

Name: _____ Phone: _____

UPS Address:_____.

City:_____ State:_____ Zip: _____

We Offer a 100% Money Back Guarantee

If for any reason, within 30 days after you receive your order, you are not 100% satisfied, you may return the items, and you will get a 100% refund — no questions asked.